100

THINGS TO DO IN

TACOMA

BEFORE YOU

DIE

100

THINGS TO DO IN

TACOMA

BEFORE YOU

DIE

● ●

PEGGY CLEVELAND

REEDY PRESS

Copyright © 2022 by Reedy Press, LLC
Reedy Press
PO Box 5131
St. Louis, MO 63139, USA
www.reedypress.com

Library of Congress Control Number: 2022936986

ISBN: 9781681063935

Design by Jill Halpin

All photos are courtesy of the author or believed to be in the public domain unless otherwise noted.

Printed in the United States of America
22 23 24 25 26   5 4 3 2 1

DEDICATION

To my husband, Rich, who has encouraged my writing dreams from the beginning.

CONTENTS

Preface xiii

Acknowledgments xv

Food and Drink

1. Be Stunned by the Views at Copper & Salt Northwest Kitchen 2

2. Wake Up with Art during Brunch at the Art House Café 3

3. Slink Into the Speakeasy Vibe at El Gaucho 4

4. Search Out Jan Parker Cookery 5

5. Support the Environment at Table 47 6

6. Devour a Doughnut at Legendary Doughnuts 7

7. Sip a Cup of Joe in a Historic Setting at Topside Coffee Cabin.................... 8

8. Explore This Asian Market and Try Something New at Pal Do World 10

9. Elevate Your Steakhouse Experience at Stanford's Steak........................... 11

10. Savor Farm-to-Table Bites at Incalmo 12

11. Delight in the Sizzling Hot Stones at Cuerno Bravo 13

12. Scream for Ice Cream at Ice Cream Social.. 14

13. Dig into Tasty Burgers at the Iconic Frisko Freeze 16

14. Get Bombed at Tibbitts Fernhill 18

15. Explore New Tastes at New Gangnam BBQ.. 19

• •

16. Chomp Down on a Gourmet Hot Dog at the Red Hot 20

17. Explore the Eclectic Food Offerings in Parkland 22

18. Pack a Picnic from the Metropolitan Market 24

19. Eat a Hearty Breakfast at the Homestead Restaurant & Bakery 26

20. Try a Ruston Way Restaurant 28

Music and Entertainment

21. Be Serenaded on the Gig Harbor Gondola 32

22. Sway to Live Music at the Steilacoom Farmers Market 33

23. Chill Out to Live Music at the Spanish Ballroom 34

24. Drive a Ford Model T at the LeMay Collections at Marymount 36

25. See More from Your Feet Than from Your Seat
with a Tacoma Brewery Row Tour 38

26. Escape from Mayan Ruins at Escape Hour 39

27. Get Serious about Gaming at Ocean5 40

28. Rock Out at the Tacoma Dome 41

29. Watch a Variety of Events at the Emerald Queen Event Center 42

30. Take in a Show at Tacoma's Theater District 43

31. Fill Your Soul at ALMA 44

32. Blow a Work of Art at the Tacoma Glass Studio 45

33. Dive Into This Dive Bar at Bob's Java Jive 46

34. Party at Jazzbones 47

35. Find Your Inner Lumberjack at Bullseye Lane Axe Throwing 48

36. Find a Treasure at Hi-Voltage Records and Books 49

37. Sing Along with Dueling Musicians at Keys on Main 50

38. Laugh Out Loud at the Tacoma Comedy Club 51

39. Play Some Games at Dorky's Arcade 52

40. Discover Handcrafted Treasures at Tacoma's Night Market 53

Sports and Recreation

41. Take Me Out to the Ball Game with the Tacoma Rainiers 56

42. Experience a Traditional Links Golf Course at Chambers Bay 57

43. Explore Land and Sea at Point Defiance Zoo and Aquarium 58

44. Take the Ferry to Explore Anderson Island 59

45. Hike the Tacoma Narrows Bridge 60

46. Paddle Your Way around the Thea Foss Waterway 62

47. Rent an Electric Bike to Explore Point Defiance Five Mile Drive 63

48. Hike the Sequalitchew Creek Trail 64

49. Discover the Outdoors in an Urban Nature Preserve
at the Tacoma Nature Center 65

50. Hope for the Environment at Dune Peninsula Park 66

51. Learn the History of Indigenous People on the Puyallup Tribe Walk 67

52. Explore Farrell Marsh 68

53. Explore the Beauty of Chambers Creek Regional Park 69

54. Go See Some Snow at Crystal Mountain Resort 70

55. Learn about Pacific Northwest Animals at Northwest Trek 72

56. Discover Fort Steilacoom Park 74

57. Go Forest Bathing in McCormick Forest Park 76

58. Pick Some Blueberries at Charlotte's Blueberry Park 77

59. Beachcomb Along Puget Sound 78

60. Test Your Mountain Biking Skills at Swan Creek Park 80

Culture and History

61. Wonder at Molten Glass at the Museum of Glass 84

62. Make Some Art at the Tacoma Art Museum 85

63. Walk through Time at the Washington State History Museum 86

64. Discover the Buffalo Soldiers Museum 87

65. Get Awestruck on the Chihuly Bridge of Glass 88

66. Reflect on Mistakes of the Past at theTacoma
Chinese Reconciliation Park 89

67. Immerse Yourself in Maritime History at the Foss Waterway Seaport 90

68. Explore a Neighborhood Business District 91

69. Jump Back in Time at the Fort Nisqually Living History Museum 92

70. Learn about Military History at the Lewis Army Museum 94

71. Discover What Life Was Like in a Company Town
at the Dupont Historical Museum 96

72. Discover Chihuly at Union Station 98

73. Become an Honorary Lightkeeper at Browns Point Lighthouse Park 100

74. Stay in a Tudor Gothic Castle at Thornewood Castle 101

75. Tour the Art Collection at the Stunning Hotel Murano.......................... 102

76. Immerse in History at the Job Carr
Cabin Museum at Old Town Park 104

77. Learn the Legend of Galloping Gertie at the
Harbor History Museum 105

78. Be Intrigued at the Karpeles Manuscript Museum 106

79. Be Enthralled with the Rare Plants at the
W.W. Seymour Botanical Conservatory 107

80. Visit the Steilacoom Historical Museum 108

Shopping and Fashion

81. Shop till You Drop at Pine and Moss.. 112

82. Discover Feel-Good Fashion at 27 West... 113

83. Explore Korean Shopping at Shin Shin 114

84. Wander Watson's Greenhouse and Nursery 115

85. Don't Get Lost at Freighthouse Square.. 116

86. Shop Local at the Point Ruston Public Market....................................... 118

87. Visit Uptown Gig Harbor for Upscale Shopping.................................... 119

88. Support a Collection of Local, Family-Owned Businesses 120

89. Give Back with a Purchase at Compass Rose Tacoma............................ 122

90. Pop In to Tickled Pink for Fun, Inspired Shopping............................... 123

91. Get Lost Exploring at Sanford and Son Antiques 124

92. Cure Your Sweet Tooth at the Brown and Haley Factory Store 125

93. Treat Yourself at Johnson Candy Company 126

94. Discover Pacific Northwest Products 127

95. Lose Yourself among the Shelves at the Tacoma Book Center 128

96. Discover a Vintage Treasure at D. Haberdashery 129

97. Find Your Next Read at King's Books 130

98. Support Local Artists at the 253 Collective Art Gallery 131

99. Craft a Masterpiece at Tinkertopia 132

100. Find a Treasure at Tricky's Pop Culture Emporium 133

Activities by Season 135

Suggested Itineraries 139

Index 141

PREFACE

Tacoma has long sat in the shadow of its more famous neighbor Seattle when it comes to being a tourist destination. No more, I say! Reedy Press is bringing national attention to this hidden gem of a city. Not only is this such an interesting and eclectic city to visit, it is also a very special place to make your home. After growing up as a Navy brat, serving 12 years in the Army, and then becoming a military spouse, I have moved 33 times. After living all over the US and the world, I finally found my "forever home" in this lovely area.

Mountain, city, sea, not many towns can offer all three. Due to its location overlooking the Puget Sound and just a 90-minute drive to Mount Rainier, Tacoma does. You can hike the mountain in the morning, kayak in the sound in the afternoon, and take in a Broadway show in Tacoma's theater district in the evening. I love that you can drive around the city and discover neighborhoods each with their own small business districts. Community is important here and people support each other, especially our small shops, restaurants, and service businesses.

Coming up with 100 things to do here was not difficult; it was narrowing it down to 100 that was the challenge. I reached out to a good cross section of people from Tacoma to provide input for my list. We have such a diverse community, and I wanted the book to reflect that.

• •

art.
POINT RUSTON
ANITA SCHOLLER
" GAIA "

ACKNOWLEDGMENTS

First, I would like to acknowledge the Coast Salish People, who were the first settlers of the land that is now Tacoma and Pierce County, as well as their ancestors the Puyallup, Nisqually, Squaxin, Steilacoom, and Muckleshoot Indian Tribes. Thank you to Matt Wakefield, who helped me discover Tacoma's hidden gems. Kris Hay's input was invaluable to the Food and Drink section. Look for her upcoming cookbook *Tacoma Aroma: Savor the Flavor.* To the teams at Pretty Gritty Tours and *Grit City* magazine who share their deep love of the history and tales of our interesting city with their tours and articles. Thanks to Adrian Milanio, a local musician, and Danno Presents, an entertainment company, for their help with the Music and Entertainment section. Many thanks to Corey Dembeck for capturing the beauty of Tacoma in his photo for the book cover. I'd also like to acknowledge the scrappy, small, local businesses featured in this book that make Tacoma such a special place and the city that embraced and supported them during the COVID-19 pandemic.

FOOD AND DRINK

BE STUNNED
BY THE VIEWS AT COPPER & SALT NORTHWEST KITCHEN

Prepare to be stunned by the gorgeous views from the dining room at Copper & Salt Northwest Kitchen. Breathtaking views of Commencement Bay and the Olympic Mountains from the floor-to-ceiling windows add to the ambience, and you might even see an orca breach the water from your table. How cool is that! Sip a craft cocktail infused with the freshest of local ingredients before indulging in artisan dishes that capture the spirit of the Northwest. This is real food sourced from local farmers and makers, then creatively prepared for a very memorable meal. Make sure to try the burrata starter, which takes fresh creamy cheese and garnishes it with seasonal fruits or vegetables. So simple and so tasty.

5125 Grand Loop, Ruston, 253-319-8290
copperandsaltnw.com

WAKE UP
WITH ART DURING BRUNCH AT THE ART HOUSE CAFÉ

Located in the Stadium District made famous in the movie *10 Things I Hate About You*, this darling café is where locals go for brunch. It is insanely popular, so plan to arrive early to snag a coveted table. The café is adorned with rotating artwork from Pacific Northwest artists. The scratch-made cuisine coming out of this kitchen is seriously yummy. The breakfast pizza is a work of culinary art. Slathered with garlic oil and topped with parmesan, Monterey jack, prosciutto, house sausage, grilled onion, garlic, and three cage-free eggs, and then finished with fresh chives, it tastes as good as it looks. The bacon and Beecher's biscuit is more of a pastry stuffed with candied applewood-smoked bacon, Beecher's (a Seattle cheesemaker) Flagship white cheddar, and grilled onion, then topped with a sunny-side-up egg.

111 N Tacoma Ave., 253-212-2011
arthousecafe.com

SLINK INTO THE SPEAKEASY VIBE
AT EL GAUCHO

El Gaucho consistently ranks as one of Tacoma's top restaurants and is the go-to joint for special occasions. It is known for its impeccable service from the time you walk in the door as well as the quality of the ingredients it uses. The specialty is steak, and it truly is special when you see the attention to detail that goes into sourcing the beef. El Gaucho is one of a few elite restaurants serving Niman Ranch All-Natural Certified Angus Beef steaks, which are among the top 1.5 percent of all beef. It is so tender you can almost cut it with a fork. In addition, the company has its own farm for produce. All this adds up to an outstanding meal. Order something prepared tableside, whether the famed Caesar salad or a flaming dessert. Truly memorable. Make sure to check out upcoming events. These are high-end dining experiences with chef tasting menus perfectly paired with wines or, depending on the event, top-shelf tequilas.

2119 Pacific Ave., 253-272-1510
elgaucho.com/elgauchotacoma/

SEARCH OUT
JAN PARKER COOKERY

Named *South Sound* magazine's best chef in 2020, Jan Parker has some serious culinary skills she uses to craft a fusion cuisine combining her Filipinx culture with Pacific Northwest local ingredients. Before you can enjoy her food, though, you must find her. With no brick-and-mortar restaurant, she serves up fresh and distinct food from her mobile kitchen stand at community farmers markets in season, pop-ups at neighboring restaurants, and other venues. She has a cult following in Tacoma, and her food is a must for any foodie. Parker learned classic European techniques at the Seattle Art Institute, but today she draws her influences from the flavors of the Philippines. Make sure to try anything she makes with pork belly or ube, a purple yam. Her fried rice takes this simple dish to a whole new level of yumminess. There is so much more to Filipinx cooking than lumpia! Parker also offers cooking classes throughout the year for those wanting to learn more about Filipino cooking.

janparkercookery@gmail.com, 206-751-5318
janparkercookery.com

SUPPORT THE ENVIRONMENT
AT TABLE 47

Located in an upscale bowling alley and laser tag venue, Table 47 is a pleasant surprise. This farm-to-table restaurant takes reducing their environmental footprint to a whole new level. From the busy worm farm in the basement composting scraps to the geothermal heating and cooling, this is a business that is passionate about the environment. Planet-friendly food is sourced from local farmers who share the same values, while microgreens are grown right in the restaurant. What this means for you is a fresh, flavorful meal. Simple comfort foods such as flatbreads and burgers become a gourmet treat when prepared with fresh, local ingredients. Craft cocktails, local beer, and a simple but well-thought-out wine list enhance the meal. Once you are full, head into Ocean5 to work off the calories with bowling or a game of laser tag.

5268 Point Fosdick Dr., 253-857-4777
T47.com

DEVOUR A DOUGHNUT
AT LEGENDARY DOUGHNUTS

So yummy! These doughnuts really are legendary and the most creative you will find anywhere. Can doughnuts be art? These handcrafted creations sure are. The most popular is the Oprah bar, a raised bar doughnut frosted with maple and topped with freshly cooked bacon. Legendary is also known for its innovation "the doughsant," which is a croissant–doughnut fusion that is more of a dessert than a breakfast treat. There are 30–35 treats in the case each day, made fresh daily from premium ingredients. The selection includes those named after famous people and inspired by candy bars such as the Almond Joy and the Snickers bar. Adults will love the boozy balls, which are raised, glazed ball-shape doughnuts filled with BSB (local Heritage Distilling's Brown Sugar Bourbon) or Bailey's Cream. If sweet is not your thing, try a grilled doughnut panini, a "doughnut bun" filled with savory meats and cheeses.

2602 6th Ave., 253-327-1327
legendarydoughnuts.com

SIP A CUP OF JOE
IN A HISTORIC SETTING
AT TOPSIDE COFFEE CABIN

This darling coffee shop features a quaint beach-cabin vibe that locals love during Washington's gray rainy season. Coffee is a necessity in Tacoma, and the small, local shops are the best. Located in historic downtown Steilacoom, the Topside Coffee Cabin will charm you from the moment you walk in the door and smell the homemade baked goods prepared fresh each day. Free Wi-Fi and cozy seating make this the perfect spot for a coffee break. The daily quiche is divine with its flaky crust and savory filling and makes a great light lunch. On a nice day grab your coffee to go and walk down the hill to Pioneer Orchard Park for stunning views of Puget Sound and the Olympic Mountains.

Topside Coffee Cabin
215 Wilkes St., Suite 102, Steilacoom
253-244-7190
topsidebargrill.com/topside-coffee-cabin

Bluebeard Café & Roastery
2201 6th Ave., Tacoma
253-272-5600
Bluebeardcoffery.com

EXPLORE THIS ASIAN MARKET
AND TRY SOMETHING NEW AT PAL DO WORLD

Locals in the know head to the last restaurant in the Pal Do World food court, the House of Mandoo, which serves only one thing: freshly made mandoo. These fist-sized dumplings are generously filled with spicy pork, regular pork, or bean curd. The dough is light and fluffy, and you can often see it being handmade, then filled and steamed to perfection. This gastronomic delight is a perfect starter while you wait for your meal from the other vendors. Pair your mandoo with Chinese, Japanese, or Korean meals from other restaurants in the food court. Most are served with fresh banchan, which are traditional side dishes such as kimchi. After your meal, explore the market, which includes a bakery, ginseng retail shop, and a Korean grocery store that has tanks for fresh seafood.

9701 S Tacoma Way, Lakewood, 253-581-7800
facebook.com/houseofmandoo

ELEVATE YOUR STEAKHOUSE EXPERIENCE
AT STANFORD'S STEAK

Forget the white tablecloths. Stanford's Steak is a modern take on a traditional steakhouse. It is family friendly yet still very elegant. A gorgeous bar dominates the space while the décor suggests the Great Gatsby with the Art Deco vibe. The atmosphere is vibrant and fun. The food is everything you would expect from a classic American steakhouse with some creative culinary surprises thrown in. You'll find an Asian influence in some of the dishes such as the ahi tuna poke. For a true splurge try the ginormous 30-ounce tomahawk ribeye. This gorgeous bone-in ribeye is Angus beef that is marbled to perfection. Stanford's Steak also has a very popular happy hour with some great food options that make a perfect snack after exploring Tacoma's Museum District. The craft cocktails are creative and reflect the talented bartenders.

1502 Pacific Ave., 253-352-0030
stanfordssteak.com

SAVOR FARM-TO-TABLE BITES
AT INCALMO

Incalmo is one of the newer restaurants in Tacoma's dining scene serving up tasty farm-to-table pasta, pizza, and Italian bites in a beautiful setting. The name Incalmo comes from a glass-fusing technique and is appropriate for the restaurant's location in the Museum of Glass. The floor-to-ceiling windows also seem to fuse the indoor and outdoor spaces to make a bright dining venue. When the weather warms up, there is outdoor dining. It is the perfect destination for coffee and pastries after a morning tour of the museum or a great lunch spot after exploring downtown outdoor art installations. The Italian-style taverna's fresh, organic produce is sourced from Zestful Gardens, a local farm, to make their sauces and salads. Locally foraged mushrooms are a popular ingredient in this area, and Incalmo purchases locally foraged mushrooms from Adam's Mushrooms, a neighboring purveyor, to create their wild mushroom rigatoni.

1801 Dock St., 253-284-4747
thetabletacoma.com/incalmo

DELIGHT IN THE SIZZLING HOT STONES
AT CUERNO BRAVO

Cuerno Bravo Prime Steakhouse and Cantina creates a whole new type of steakhouse experience with influences from Mexico and Argentina. This is a sensory dining experience with the sizzling sounds from the wood-fired kitchen, the smells of freshly grilled beef wafting through the air, and the sight of a sizzling, hearth-heated stone served with a freshly cooked Wagyu steak. David Orozco, the owner, is obsessed with premium beef, and it shows, with USDA prime, American Wagyu, Australian Wagyu, and, at the highest end, Japanese Wagyu. This will be the best steak you have eaten in your life. There are a variety of options for ordering so you can have an affordable meal or go all out for a special occasion. Normally a simple baked potato is not worth mentioning, but Cuerno Bravo serves a behemoth that can easily serve four as a side dish. It is perfectly baked and seasoned, then topped with smoked bacon, a four-cheese blend, Mexican crema, and Wagyu carne asada. Divine! Some people even order it as a meal.

616 St. Helens Ave., 253-328-6688
cuernobravo.com

SCREAM FOR ICE CREAM
AT ICE CREAM SOCIAL

Ice Cream Social takes this simple dessert to a whole new level of yumminess. You can smell the freshly baking waffle cones well before you enter the shop. Layla Isaac created Ice Cream Social because she wanted to make something that would bring a smile to people's faces, and everybody loves ice cream. She is a self-taught ice cream maker who crafts her unique flavors from natural, local ingredients. Ice Cream Social has a loyal following due to its great-tasting product. Quality ingredients really make a difference. There are three shops in Tacoma, but the one located at Point Ruston will give you the best experience. There is nothing like ordering a crispy waffle cone filled with your favorite flavors and taking it out to the waterfront to stroll while enjoying this delectable treat. There are also plenty of benches with scenic views for miles.

5107 Main St., Ruston, 253-507-5448
icecreamsocialtacoma.com

Proctor
2521 N Proctor, 253-327-1803

Tacoma
1110 M.L.K. Jr. Way, 253-327-1660

DIG INTO TASTY BURGERS
AT THE ICONIC FRISKO FREEZE

The retro style of this 1950s iconic landmark will take you back in time. It is Tacoma's most renowned burger joint. It is still owned by descendants of the original owner. You'll find everyone from moms in fancy cars to high schoolers in pickup trucks eating here. Drive up or head to the walk-up window to order from the simple menu of burgers, fries, and shakes. The burgers are hot, juicy messes with a secret sauce, pickles, onions, ketchup, and lettuce all wrapped up in a wax bag. These are thin patties that cook quick with a subtle crispness, so make sure to order a double. Get plenty of napkins, because the only dining space is in your car. On busy Saturday nights this place is hopping, and you may have to wait a bit, but the burgers are so worth the wait.

1201 Division Ave., 253-272-6843

GET BOMBED
AT TIBBITTS FERNHILL

Get bombed not on alcohol but on food. It's rare to find a unique dish for the breakfast game but Chef Shawn Tibbitts has done it with his lobster bomb. It is one of the most unusual but tasty breakfast creations you will ever eat. He starts with a toasted bread bowl, then loads it up with champagne-soaked lobster, candied bacon, Yukon gold potatoes, sherry fennel, scrambled eggs, avocado, and farm-fresh greens, all smothered in a lemony hollandaise sauce. What makes it so amazing is he cooks it all on camp stove–type burners in a teeny, tiny kitchen. The restaurant is very small, with just a few tables, so reservations are a must. Tibbitts has a big heart, and it shows through the love he puts into preparing each dish. His friendly touch comes across as he takes time to visit tables and greet his guests.

8237 S Park Ave., 253-327-1334
tibbittsfernhill.com

EXPLORE NEW TASTES
AT NEW GANGNAM BBQ

If you aren't familiar with Korean food and culture, do yourself a favor and try Korean barbeque. The New Gangnam BBQ is in the heart of the Lakewood International district also known as Korea Town. The restaurant serves Korean-style barbecue that you cook at your table, which is equipped with a gas grill. You can order from the menu or just go with the all-you-can-eat option. Order the types of meat you wish to cook from the list and then, next thing you know, a server will roll a cart over and begin placing a variety of banchan (Korean side dishes), a bowl of cooked rice, soy sauce, and a bean paste on your table. Make sure to order the bulgogi, which is a marinated beef that is so tasty. Cook the meat over the grill and then eat separately or take a lettuce leaf, fill it with rice, meat, and pickled vegetable from the banchan, and top it with bean paste before eating it like a taco. Most of the patrons are Korean, which says a lot about the authenticity of the restaurant.

9104 S Tacoma Way, Lakewood, 253-581-1200

CHOMP DOWN
ON A GOURMET HOT DOG
AT THE RED HOT

This Tacoma institution is in the vibrant Sixth Avenue District, a hip area of local restaurants, bars, and shops. The creative geniuses working the kitchen have elevated the lowly hot dog to a whole new level of dining sophistication. The extensive menu includes an amazing selection of hot dogs, sausages, and even vegan fare. You can order a classic or try something new. The "Whole Lotta Rosie" loads a bun up with Rosemary-chicken sausage, remoulade, white cheddar, grilled onions, and arugula. So unique. Every Thursday, the Red Hot rolls out a new or seasonal creation so there is always something new to try. Desserts consist of old-time favorites like the MoonPie and Cracker Jacks. This is an over-21 establishment with a great selection of Pacific Northwest craft beer on tap. If you have little ones, takeout is available.

2914 6th Ave., 253-779-0229
redhottacoma.com

EXPLORE THE ECLECTIC FOOD OFFERINGS
IN PARKLAND

Parkland is an interesting suburb of Tacoma with some surprising food offerings. On the upscale end you have Marzano, where owners Elisa and Brian Marzano take the Italian cuisine from northern Italy and infuse it with ingredients from Pacific Northwest artisans and small farmers to create something magical. This place is insanely popular, so make a reservation well in advance, especially for busy weekends. Don't let the humble strip mall–exterior deter you from visiting the Parkland Place Bakery and Bistro. Caterer Susan Krogh has a cult following for her luscious cheesecakes. After being a regular on the farmers market–circuit, she now has a storefront with five-star reviews. It is a perfect place for lunch and to grab some pastries for later. The Marvel Food and Deli and its sister business, the Marvel Bay Café, provide authentic European foods from Russia, Ukraine, Hungary, Germany, Italy, France, and many more. For a restaurant experience, dine at the café or get food to go from the market. You'll find piroshki, borscht, goulash, and a variety of European treats. The market is worth visiting for the candy aisle alone. Yes, a full grocery aisle dedicated to candy by the pound from all over Europe.

Marzano
516 Garfield St. S, 253-537-4191
dinemarzano.com

Parkland Place Bakery and Bistro
14906 Pacific Ave. S, Parkland, 253-301-4658
parklandplacebakerybistro.com

Marvel Food and Deli/Marvel Bay Café
301 133rd St. S, 253-537-1008
marvelfoodanddeli.com
marvelbaycafe.com

PACK A PICNIC
FROM THE METROPOLITAN MARKET

The Metropolitan Market is a chain of upscale markets that will delight foodies with premium ingredients and local products. With so many great options for both hot and cold takeout, it is no wonder so many visit just for a meal. According to the *Seattle Times* food writer Tan Vinh, "The Met Market prime rib is arguably the most underrated sandwich in Seattle." You can second that for Tacoma. The all-day tradition of flame-roasting prime rib to perfection began 20 years ago. Thinly sliced and piled high on a crispy, fresh baguette topped with horseradish sauce and served with au jus for dipping. Divine! For dessert you can't miss the "Cookie." This delectable mass of a chocolate chip cookie oozes warm Belgian chocolate, both semisweet and bittersweet Callebaut, from its buttery goodness. Baked fresh all day and placed on warming stones, you can enjoy this treat like it just came out of the oven all day. The perfect ending to a gourmet, grocery store meal. Grab picnic fixings and head to Point Defiance Park for an al fresco meal.

TIP

If you prefer to eat at the Met, it has a heated outdoor patio with seating. Then you can explore the shops in the Proctor District.

LOCATIONS

Tacoma
2420 N. Proctor St., 253-761-3663
metropolitan-market.com

Gig Harbor
5010 Point Fosdick Dr., Gig Harbor,
253-858-4842
metropolitan-market.com

EAT A HEARTY BREAKFAST
AT THE HOMESTEAD
RESTAURANT & BAKERY

This is not your fancy, hoity-toity brunch spot but rather where people go for a big, stick-to-your-ribs breakfast. You can't miss the big, red barn that houses the family-owned Homestead Restaurant & Bakery, which has dished up ginormous breakfasts for over 30 years. The focus is comfort food from recipes and ingredients that reflect the family's heritage. The vintage Western theme is fun, and tables have screens that scroll through photos of menu items. It is so hard to decide, so here are a few suggestions to narrow down your choices. They are famed for serving chicken-fried steak nine different ways. One of the more infamous ways is the "Squatch" as in "Big Foot." Homemade fry bread is slathered with Alfredo sauce, then topped with three eggs scrambled with bell peppers, onions, mushrooms, a half-pound chicken-fried steak, and more Alfredo sauce. With cinnamon rolls the size of your head, the "Wagon Wheel" is more than enough to share. The Homestead's renowned cinnamon rolls are sliced and made into French toast, which is then stuffed with ham, bacon, crispy hash browns, and American cheese, then drizzled with icing.

7837 S Tacoma Way, 253-476-9000
homesteadwa.com

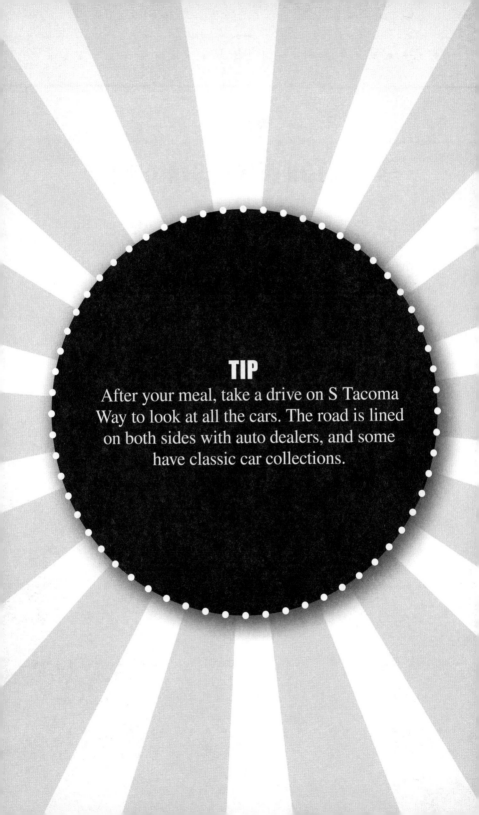

TIP

After your meal, take a drive on S Tacoma Way to look at all the cars. The road is lined on both sides with auto dealers, and some have classic car collections.

TRY
A RUSTON WAY RESTAURANT

Stretching from Point Ruston to Old Town Tacoma, Ruston Way is the place to cruise with waterfront views of Puget Sound and the Olympic Mountains. It is also home to some of the best seafood restaurants in the city as well as a tavern famed for its deep-dish pizza. Both the Lobster Shop and Duke's Seafood offer wonderful selections of Pacific Northwest seafood. The Lobster Shop is a more upscale choice. You can't get more romantic than a sunset dinner here. Duke's is famed for its chowders. If you can't decide, order a dinghy sampler, choosing one to four of the award-winning chowders. Katie Downs is a family-owned business and one of the first on Ruston Way. This over-21 establishment has a lively atmosphere and an eclectic menu offering everything from seafood to burgers and pizza with to-die-for waterfront and mountain views.

Duke's Seafood
3327 Ruston Way, 253-752-5444
dukesseafood.com

Lobster Shop
4015 Ruston Way, 253-759-2165
lobstershop.com

Katie Downs Waterfront Tavern
3211 Ruston Way, 253-756-0771
katiedowns.com

Brian the Pianist Is a Volunteer

MUSIC
AND ENTERTAINMENT

BE SERENADED
ON THE GIG HARBOR GONDOLA

This is not your average harbor cruise. Climb aboard an authentic Venetian gondola named Nelly after the original owner's mother. John Synco, the gondolier and owner, shares tales of Gig Harbor history and serenades guests as he propels the boat through the water utilizing Venetian rowing, a style that uses just one oar. The harbor is scenic rain or shine, but a clear day provides stunning views of Mount Rainier and the tiny Gig Harbor Lighthouse. The gondola is surprisingly spacious and can carry six passengers. It is truly a unique way to explore this lovely body of water. You can preorder an appetizer box or bring your own food and drinks. I suggest your favorite bottle of Washington State wine. Truly a unique experience.

Meet at the Gig Harbor Marina
3117 Harborview Dr., Gig Harbor, 253-432-0052
gigharborgondola.com

SWAY TO LIVE MUSIC
AT THE STEILACOOM FARMERS MARKET

The Steilacoom Farmers Market is a very popular local event that draws visitors from all over the area. It is held every Wednesday afternoon during the summer months in the historic town of Steilacoom. The more than 80 vendors are local farmers, artists, specialty merchants, and food vendors. It runs 3–7 p.m. and the live music kicks off at 6 p.m. in Pioneer Orchard Park. The bandstand overlooks the sound and is a very scenic spot to listen to live music. Take some time to read the interpretive signs, which provide geographical information. On a clear day you can see the Olympic Mountains. Bring your own chair, set up early, and then head to the market to pick up something for dinner from one of the food trucks or other vendors. The Steilacoom's Summer Concert Series offers a different type of music each week.

207 Wilkes St., Steilacoom
facebook.com/steilacoomfarmersmarket/

CHILL OUT TO LIVE MUSIC
AT THE SPANISH BALLROOM

The Spanish Bar and Ballroom at McMenamins Elks Temple is the place to be for live music in Tacoma. Offering a variety of genres in this grand space typically Wednesday through Sunday each week. Built in 1916, the Elks Temple was once the site of ballroom dancing and other events. The building is on the National Register of Historic Places and is now reimagined as a vibrant gathering place. With grand chandeliers and ornate trim, the Spanish Ballroom can hold 700, which is enough of a crowd for high energy but still intimate in size. Check out the upstairs bar, which overlooks the ballroom for an elevated view of the stage. The live music concerts feature some of the top bands in the country with a fantastic, diverse schedule. Country, rock, pop, and even acoustic guitar artists appear on the monthly schedules. Most nights the music is free, but check the schedule for ticketed concerts.

565 Broadway, 253-300-8754
mcmenamins.com/elks-temple/spanish-ballroom

TIP

Make sure to check out the Spanish Steps, which are adjacent to McMenamins Elks Temple. The steps, constructed in 1916 to connect Broadway and Commerce Street, were modeled after the more famous Scalinata di Spagna (Spanish Steps) in Rome. The City of Tacoma recognized the historical importance and restored the steps in 2011.

DRIVE A FORD MODEL T
AT THE LEMAY COLLECTIONS
AT MARYMOUNT

Fans of the Fox Business series *Strange Inheritance* will be familiar with Harold LeMay's collection of over 3,000 cars. It was listed in the *Guinness Book of World Records 1997* as the largest privately owned car collection in the world. You truly experience the sheer immensity of this collection when you tour the family's museum, which contains the bulk of the collection. If you time it right, you can book a "Model T Experience" and learn the history of this famous car and how Henry Ford's "Tin Lizzie" made car ownership available to the masses. The car has three foot pedals, one hand lever, and two hand controls, making it a challenge to drive. You will receive instruction, and once you have the hang of it you can drive around the historic Marymount Academy campus with its beautiful Douglas fir forest.

325 152nd St. E, 253-272-2336
lemaymarymount.org/

TIP
Make sure to tour the grounds during your visit and explore the Rodin Sculpture Garden, which features some of his famous works, like *The Thinker*, cast from the original molds.

SEE MORE
FROM YOUR FEET THAN FROM YOUR SEAT WITH A TACOMA BREWERY ROW TOUR

Pretty Gritty Tours is a group of local guides, artists, and a historian who bring Tacoma, also known as the "Grit City," to life. The Tacoma Brewery Row tour gives you the best of both worlds, the opportunity to learn some of the scandalous stories and history of the city, and taste the great local beer. The tour starts at the E9 Brewery in the heart of Tacoma's brewery row, and you will utilize the free Link light rail that meanders through downtown Tacoma and is a fabulous way to embark on a pub crawl. You will visit four local breweries and enjoy beer and snacks during the tour. Each guide is a Tacoma local and a gifted storyteller. This is not a dry, boring tour but a super lively one with bawdy tales, Tacoma history, and interesting facts about beer. Pretty Gritty Tours offers a variety of historical tours around the area. If beer is not your thing, maybe try a Sweets Tour.

253-480-4074
prettygrittytours.com/

ESCAPE FROM MAYAN RUINS
AT ESCAPE HOUR

Escape Hour Gig Harbor has arguably the top escape rooms in the state. This is not a low-budget experience but more like a ride at Disney World. The owners of this family-owned business are amusement-park aficionados and wanted their escape rooms to have that feeling. When you enter the Curse of the Mayan Ruins you are immediately enveloped in the sights and sounds that transport you to South America and undiscovered Mayan ruins. Inspired by the Indiana Jones movies, this room quickly immerses you in the experience. Work your way through dimly lit corridors and maze-like hallways searching for a way out by solving puzzles or tasks. It's a race against time to see if you can uncover all the clues to escape the curse before your luck runs out. The escape rooms are challenging but solvable.

3212 50th St. Ct., #104, Gig Harbor, 253-314-0107
escapehourgigharbor.com

GET SERIOUS ABOUT GAMING
AT OCEAN5

Ocean5 is an upscale entertainment complex that takes family-friendly fun to a whole new level. Adults will love it, too. Walking through the door into the immense lobby, you will be enthralled with the huge hanging art that resembles fish scales. There is a giant 360-degree fireplace with circular seating around it that is the perfect spot to enjoy a latte or a craft cocktail. Activities include 22 lanes of bowling with classic 10-pin or duckpin. You can even reserve a suite. The laser arena is two stories tall and can have up to 40 players per game. The modern arcade has classic favorites as well as the latest in game machines. Earn points to redeem for fabulous prizes. The latest addition to Ocean5 is the Top Golf Swing Suites. This virtual experience allows you to play your favorite golf courses. Adults will love the fully stocked bar with the best of Pacific Northwest distillers, brewers, and winemakers.

5268 Point Fosdick Dr., Gig Harbor, 253-857-7529
o5social.com

ROCK OUT
AT THE TACOMA DOME

The Tacoma Dome is the venue that hosts big crowd events. It is one of the largest wood-domed structures in the world. With the recent addition of telescopic seating, the dome hosts events for up to 21,000. Many a graduate from one of Tacoma's high schools has walked across a stage here to receive their diplomas. This is the place to see big name concerts and other world-class entertainment like monster trucks. Annual events include the Tacoma RV Show and the Tacoma Home and Garden Show. The venue has plenty of parking. If you have some time to spare, LeMay—America's Car Museum is adjacent to the Tacoma Dome and showcases a variety of automobiles, including some from the Harold LeMay Collection. The Tacoma Dome Station is the terminus for the Tacoma Link light rail, which provides an easy way to explore downtown.

2727 E D St., 253-272-3663
tacomadome.org

WATCH A VARIETY OF EVENTS
AT THE EMERALD QUEEN EVENT CENTER

Driving I-5 in Tacoma you can't miss the grand Emerald Queen Casino, with its flashing lights and billboards. The artwork and architectural features were designed by Puyallup tribal members and feature traditional and contemporary symbols of the Coast Salish. The artwork is on a scale such that you can see it from the interstate. The state-of-the-art Emerald Queen Event Center is Tacoma's newest venue for live music and has stadium seating for 1,800+. With luxurious theater-style seating and immersive audio, it takes concert going to a whole new level. Look for national concert tours, MMA fights, and other events throughout the year. Check out the casino after your concert. The $400 million property features Vegas-style gaming and has over 2,100 slots, 60 table games, and 6 dining venues. There is also a brand-new hotel on-site.

5700 Pacific Hwy. E, Fife, 253-594-7777
emeraldqueen.com/tickets/

TAKE IN A SHOW
AT TACOMA'S THEATER DISTRICT

The Tacoma Theater District is a vibrant area of the city offering world-class artists performing year-round. There is really something for everyone. The district consists of three theaters that host eight resident arts organizations. Offerings include special events, Broadway shows, ballets, symphonies, live comedy, concerts in a variety of genres, and musicals. The Pantages Theater dates to 1918 and is one of the oldest Pantages Theaters still in operation. The Rialto Theater is also historic and opened in 1918. It was originally a movie house with beautiful Beaux-Arts features that still exist today. The Theater on the Square is the newest of the three, opening in 1993. Plan a night at the theater, there are many local restaurants close by for a meal or post-show cocktails.

310 S 9th St., 253-591-5894
tacomaartslive.org

FILL YOUR SOUL
AT ALMA

ALMA means nourishment and soul and that is what this venue seeks to do. This welcoming space is a community fixture that locals love. It is more than a business, it has a purpose to celebrate arts, culture, and the Coast Salish and the Puyallup, the indigenous peoples on whose traditional lands ALMA sits. The purposeful mission at ALMA strives to uplift each individual and to be a conduit for art and cultural exchange that connects and uplifts the community. The venue hosts a variety of live music and cultural events. You'll also find plenty of artwork that adds to the experience. ALMA is renowned for its food as well, and you'll often find local chefs dining here. The dining program seeks to honor the Puyallup people by using locally sourced ingredients and traditional indigenous foodways. This really is a special place to enjoy a night out.

1322 Fawcett Ave., 253-507-7289
almatacoma.com

BLOW A WORK OF ART
AT THE TACOMA GLASS STUDIO

With Tacoma's rich heritage of glass art, you may want to try your hand at glassblowing. Husband and wife team, Mark and Jeannine, offer a glassblowing experience that is perfect for beginners. Guided by an instructor, you will have the opportunity to create a glass art piece from hot, molten glass. Pick and choose your colors and how you want them integrated into your work. Then blow and shape them into your choice of a paperweight, heart, float, ornament, or many more options. This is such a unique experience, and your glass art will be a wonderful memento from your trip. The studio also runs a shop with beautiful works of glass art from local artisans. In the fall, the Tacoma Glassblowing Studio sponsors Northwest Glass Pumpkin Patches, which feature up to 2,000 works of handblown glass pumpkins by local glass artisans. These glass art pumpkins are highly collectible and sought after by locals who look forward to this event each year for the chance to add on to their collections.

114 S 23rd St., 253-383-3499
tacomaglassblowing.com

DIVE INTO THIS DIVE BAR
AT BOB'S JAVA JIVE

This iconic coffeepot-shaped building built in 1927 is home to Bob's Java Jive, a Tacoma landmark that gives new meaning to the term "dive bar." When the COVID-19 pandemic took its toll, people from around the world contributed money and labor to save this much-beloved coffeepot on the National Register of Historic Places. Enjoy karaoke most nights with some seriously good locals belting out tunes. Before their success, the Ventures, famed for the song "Wipe Out," were the house band. Rumor has it, Nirvana either played here or was rejected to play here—that is the great thing about a legendary venue, the stories and rumors. The interior still has remnants of the tiki hut décor popular in the 1950s, although the jungle vines are gone due to the fire code, as are the monkeys Java and Jive.

2102 S Tacoma Way, 253-475-9843
facebook.com/bobsjavajive

PARTY
AT JAZZBONES

When you ask a local where to see live music, Jazzbones is sure to come up in the conversation. Located in the popular Sixth Avenue District, Jazzbones will delight live music–lovers. Check their calendar for upcoming events. You'll find local, regional, and national artists performing a variety of musical styles. Themed music nights and even rockaroke, which is karaoke performed with a live band. How cool is that! Jazzbones is also a nightclub with the hottest DJs and a restaurant with a surprisingly eclectic menu, offering up bar food as well as vegan options such as a cauliflower filet. There is even a mojito-themed pizza. For those who want their own space, book the private balcony, which offers great views of the band or DJ performing.

2803 6th Ave., 253-396-9169
jazzbones.com

FIND YOUR INNER LUMBERJACK
AT BULLSEYE LANE AXE THROWING

Forged axe throwing has become very popular in the Pacific Northwest. It is a deceptively simple activity where you fling an axe with all your might at a target. The challenge is to get the axe to stick in the target so you can score. Bullseye Lane has trained and certified coaches who take the time to demonstrate the proper throwing technique while taking you through a few practice runs. Then there are fun games to play on digitally projected targets, each one unique. Lanes will hold up to six people and children eight and above are welcome. A very fun change of pace instead of bowling. Bullseye Lane offers prepackaged food and nonalcoholic beverages, but you are welcome to bring in food from a nearby restaurant.

Opera Alley, 705 Court C #307, 253-627-4302
bullseyelane.com

FIND A TREASURE
AT HI-VOLTAGE RECORDS AND BOOKS

A visit to Hi-Voltage Records and Books offers more than just shopping, it is an entertainment experience. Vinyl aficionados will love that this shop is owned and operated by musicians. Customer service has a depth of music knowledge that is what makes a local record shop so great. Each week, find the latest in new vinyl releases or browse through the used vinyl and CD collection. This store has a massive collection of over 40,000 records and CDs. Everything is graded and well organized, so it is easy to find what you are looking for. Take advantage of the music knowledge and ask for a recommendation so you can enjoy a new find. Hi-Voltage recently added books to their offerings, which expands the appeal. Merchandise includes band T-shirts as well as their own label items which utilizes their cool Hi-Voltage logo.

2714 6th Ave., 253-627-4278
hivoltagerecords.com

SING ALONG
WITH DUELING MUSICIANS
AT KEYS ON MAIN

Get ready for an energetic good time with the Dueling Piano Show at Keys on Main. Talented musicians duke it out on two grand pianos on the main stage. The show is interactive, and you can throw out requests, but it will cost you $20 to get it played. Pretty much anything played on the radio in the last 65 years is game. The piano players know thousands of songs from all genres of music. See if you can stump them with a song they don't know. It is a very rowdy atmosphere encouraged by the musicians. Full bar but no food. You can order takeout to be delivered to your table or bring in your own food. Keys on Main is very popular, especially on weekends. Make sure to secure a reservation so you are not disappointed. This is an over-21 establishment, and the banter between pianists and the audience can get racy at times.

1003 Pacific Ave., 253-627-7555
tacoma.keysonmain.com

LAUGH OUT LOUD
AT THE TACOMA COMEDY CLUB

Enjoy a night out at the Tacoma Comedy Club with a rotating roster of regional and national touring comedians performing on the weekends. Prices are surprisingly affordable to see comedians you'll recognize from television. Have you ever wanted to try your hand at comedy? Check out New Talent Tuesdays and Open Mic Wednesdays. Admission is free these two nights, and you may discover the next Jerry Seinfeld or watch the worst comic ever, but, hey, it's free. This lively club also offers a full food and drink menu. Seating is cabaret style with small tables that seat four to six. Make a reservation to book the best seats and pay the lowest price on tickets. Same-day tickets are available at the door if any spots remain available.

933 Market St., 253-282-7203
tacomacomedyclub.com

PLAY SOME GAMES
AT DORKY'S ARCADE

Dorky's Arcade in downtown Tacoma is an insanely popular 1980s-style arcade with all your favorite vintage arcade games, including Donkey Kong and Defender. The interior has an industrial feel with bare brick walls adorned with graffiti murals. It is gritty, just like Tacoma. Dorky's just passed their 20th anniversary and has developed quite a following among game enthusiasts. Reviews can be found on YouTube from visitors as far away as Japan. The arcade was also featured in a national T-Mobile commercial, the proceeds from which helped make improvements to this small business. In addition to arcade games, you'll find a huge selection of vintage pinball machines, including the Addams Family, which is the bestselling pinball machine of all time. After 9 p.m. the arcade turns into a bar with plenty of beer and an over-21 crowd. The DJ booth has a killer sound system to rock out to while trying to match your '80s scores on your favorite game.

754 Pacific Ave., 253-627-4156
dorkysarcade.com

DISCOVER HANDCRAFTED TREASURES
AT TACOMA'S NIGHT MARKET

Leah Morgan created the Tacoma Night Market to bring the community together, support small businesses and artisans, and to raise money for Pacific Northwest nonprofits. What started as pop-up markets has now become a sought-after event in Tacoma. Morgan curates the vendors to create a unique event. You hear music and enjoy an eclectic selection of food vendors while meeting the artists who make up Tacoma's vibrant art scene. Great music adds to the atmosphere, making this an event, not just a shopping excursion. All ages are welcome, and it is free. Taking home an object you have purchased directly from an artist after hearing their story makes it even more special. For 2022, the night market takes place in the Foss Waterway Seaport once a month. Look for other pop-up events throughout the year.

705 Dock St.,
tacomanightmarket.com
Instagram: @tacomanightmarket

SPORTS
AND RECREATION

TAKE ME OUT TO THE BALL GAME
WITH THE TACOMA RAINIERS

There is nothing like a sunny, summer day to enjoy a baseball game. Head over to Cheney Stadium to cheer on the Tacoma Rainiers, a Triple-A affiliate of the Seattle Mariners and a member of the Triple-A West. Cheney Stadium has hosted teams since 1960. Renovations in 2010 created a state-of-the-art entertainment venue where you can watch a game from stadium seats or a luxury suite. Each summer, the Rainiers offer specialty nights at home games that bring together the local community for fun baseball excitement. Concessions include traditional ballpark favorites and seafood from Ivar's, a local chain famed for their classic fish and chips, fish tacos, chowders, and clams. They even offer the Ivar Dog, a seafood-based hot dog loaded with coleslaw and tartar sauce.

2502 S Tyler St., 253-752-7707
milb.com/tacoma

EXPERIENCE A TRADITIONAL LINKS GOLF COURSE
AT CHAMBERS BAY

Golf lovers will enjoy playing a few rounds at one of the most stunning courses in the United States. From its humble beginnings as a weed-covered gravel pit, it has become one of the top public golf courses in the nation. Chambers Bay offers one of the few links courses in the United States. Traditionalists love these courses for their resemblance to St Andrews, where golf was founded. You will feel that mystical quality playing the course with its rugged dunes and seaside grasses. The course takes advantage of the natural features of the property to create a special experience. It is rare that you can experience tournament-quality golf on a public course. Chambers Bay was host to the PGA 2015 US Open. The Grill is known for its panoramic views and draws not only golfers but savvy locals as well.

6320 Grandview Dr. W, University Place, 253-460-4653
chambersbaygold.com

EXPLORE LAND AND SEA
AT POINT DEFIANCE ZOO
AND AQUARIUM

You really get a lot of bang for your buck at the Point Defiance Zoo and Aquarium, where not only can you experience land animals but also creatures under the sea at the Pacific Seas Aquarium. It is all situated overlooking Puget Sound. The Pacific Seas Aquarium is the newest feature of the park. One of the most popular features is Baja Bay, which has a unique architectural feature that allows the sharks and marine animals to swim overhead. Although there are plenty of large mammals like the majestic elephants, kids and adults alike are drawn to the Kids Zone to watch the meerkats frolic in their habitat. There is a fun zoo-themed playground, and you can even feed the goats.

5400 N Pearl St., 253-404-3800
pdza.org

TAKE THE FERRY
TO EXPLORE ANDERSON ISLAND

Head into historic Steilacoom and hop the ferry to Anderson Island. Keep an eye out for bald eagles, harbor porpoises, and harbor seals, all of which you can often see from the ferry. Anderson Island is a small rural community, 10 percent of which is public parks. This beautiful island is relatively undeveloped, with lots of lush forests and beachfront available to explore. Head to one of Anderson Island's parks to hike or enjoy the waterfront. In the summer months, enjoy an old-fashioned swimming hole at Lowell Johnson Park, which has two swimming areas on Florence Lake. The Riviera Lakeshore Restaurant overlooks the lovely Lake Josephine, and you can see Mount Rainier peeking out in the distance. It is the perfect spot for lunch after a busy morning of exploration. Reservations are a must, since it is the only restaurant on the island.

56 Union Ave., Steilacoom, 253-588-1950
piercecountywa.gov/1793/ferry

TIP
Go to andersonislandparks.org and download the guide to Anderson Island parks.

HIKE
THE TACOMA NARROWS BRIDGE

The Tacoma Narrows Bridge is infamous for its "Galloping Gertie," where old videos show the bridge buckling and swaying before collapsing into the narrows. No worries now. The current bridge is safe and affords magnificent views of the area, including of Mount Rainier from the crest of the bridge. Park at War Memorial Park, which deserves a quick exploration of its military history exhibits. The Narrows Bridge hike follows a 3.4-mile out-and-back paved path. It is considered moderately steep with a consistent 5 percent grade peaking at 8 percent, but the intensity of the hike rewards you with its epic views. Monitor wind conditions, as it can get extremely windy through the narrows and at times it is not safe to hike the bridge.

War Memorial Park
624 N Meyers St.

TIP

Local legend has it that the King Octopus lives among the ruins of the original Tacoma Narrows Bridge. It is said to weigh 600 pounds and have massive tentacles that can grab those who explore too closely. In reality, octopuses live hiding among the ruins but top out at 50 pounds. You can see the real deal at the Point Defiance Zoo and Aquarium. Many local shops carry books and octopus toys. It is a fun story to share with children.

PADDLE YOUR WAY
AROUND THE THEA FOSS WATERWAY

How awesome is urban paddling? Rent a kayak or stand-up paddleboard at the Dock Street Marina or the Foss Harbor Marina and you'll be on your way to find out as you paddle past downtown Tacoma. The Thea Foss Waterway is a 1.5-mile-long inlet off Commencement Bay and is perfect for beginning paddlers, with its glassy still water. Amid downtown Tacoma you see plenty of landmarks during your paddle, including Old City Hall, Union Station, and the Museum of Glass. The Tacoma skyline has a pleasantly historic look, and the Murray Morgan Bridge is architecturally interesting, especially when viewed from the water. After you've worked up an appetite, check out one of the many waterfront eateries, many with outside dining on Tacoma's sunny, summer days.

1817 Dock St., 253-250-1906
dockstreetmarina.com

RENT AN ELECTRIC BIKE
TO EXPLORE POINT DEFIANCE
FIVE MILE DRIVE

Head over to Wheel Fun Rentals (you can't miss the brightly colored awnings of the surreys for rent) and check out an electric bike. They are easy to ride and will help you fly up the hills without noticing the incline. Each rental comes with a self-guided tour of the Point Ruston/Point Defiance area. Times vary but Five Mile Drive is closed to vehicle traffic for a period of time each day. This beautiful ride will take you into Point Defiance Park for a ride around the perimeter. You'll pedal past gorgeous gardens and a dense old-growth forest with huge trees. There are plenty of viewpoints to stop at and see the Tacoma Narrows, Owen Beach, Gig Harbor, and Puget Sound heading into the Port of Tacoma. As you traverse the park you can see why it has been a popular place for over 100 years. It really is the crown jewel of Metro Parks Tacoma.

5115 Grand Loop, 253-503-1487
wheelfunrentals.com/wa/tacoma/point-ruston

HIKE
THE SEQUALITCHEW CREEK TRAIL

This is the trail locals hike, some every day. It is just stunning from beginning to end. Park at Dupont City Hall, which has the only available restrooms during the trek. It begins by the interpretive signs. Once you start you are quickly enveloped in a magical forest of Douglas firs, rich green mosses, and ferns. The old railroad bed takes you 1.5 miles along a ravine gradually dropping down to Puget Sound and a rocky beach. Toward the end you'll see interpretive signs next to the saltwater marsh before crossing under a railroad by tunnel. Trains run frequently and children love to stand in the tunnel as trains roar above. From the beach you will have views of Puget Sound islands and the Olympic Mountains in the distance. Harbor porpoises and seals are often spotted from this area. The trip back is uphill, but it is a gentle slope and not too strenuous. The trail is well maintained and stroller friendly until you get to the beach, where it is very rocky.

1700 Civic Dr., DuPont, WA 98327
Wta.org/go-hiking/hikes/dupont-sequalitchew-creek

DISCOVER THE OUTDOORS
IN AN URBAN NATURE PRESERVE
AT THE TACOMA NATURE CENTER

The Tacoma Nature Center is a fun, free activity families will love. Explore the more than two miles of walking trails that meander through a forest and wetlands. Deer are often spotted as well as a variety of bird species. The flat even trail is very stroller friendly. It is hard to believe you are in the middle of town and not an epic hike when on the trails. Discovery Pond is a fun play area for children that is not your average playground. Exploring and creative play is encouraged with a boulder scramble, a snag climb, a pond with waterfalls, a log crossing, a tree house, and so much more you'll have a hard time getting the kids to leave. Indoors you will find the Interpretive Center which has interactive exhibits on wetlands, the watershed, and wildlife exhibits. The gift shop offers nature-themed gifts, toys, and tools for nature exploration.

1919 S Tyler St., 253-404-3930
tacomaparks.com
metroparkstacoma.org/place/tacoma-nature-center/

HOPE FOR THE ENVIRONMENT
AT DUNE PENINSULA PARK

Dune Peninsula is built on what was once part of the Asarco smelter site, one of the first Superfund sites and one of the most polluted areas in the country. Today the Point Defiance and Point Ruston waterfront is one of the most beautiful in the nation and a true environmental success story. Dune Peninsula is named after the book *Dune*, by native son Frank Herbert, whose plot includes a group trying to restore a planet's environment. The winding paved pedestrian loop through the peninsula was named the Frank Herbert Trail. The 11-acre park is landscaped with native drought-tolerant plants and has quickly become a popular place for walks or for just contemplating the gorgeous views of Puget Sound, local islands, Mount Rainier, and the Port of Tacoma. The Wilson Way Bridge connects Point Ruston and Point Defiance and has an overlook named "the Moment" to encourage taking some time to appreciate the beauty around you. There are six slides next to the bridge that will take you down to the marina below. Or use the adjacent steps. It has been nicknamed "Chutes and Ladders".

5361 Yacht Club Rd., 253-305-1090
metroparkstacoma.org/place/dune-peninsula/

LEARN THE HISTORY OF INDIGENOUS PEOPLE
ON THE PUYALLUP TRIBE WALK

This is a digital guided tour that is just fascinating. Download the GeoTourist app to access the tour and start in Tollefson Plaza. Your guide is Charlotte Basch, a tribal member and the historic education coordinator for the Puyallup Tribe of Indians. She will take you on a two-mile walk beginning in Tollefson Plaza and moving through downtown, sharing the history of the Puyallup and their interactions with the land and the city as you go. Tacoma was once the site of a major Puyallup village, which Basch describes via reference to the tribe's oral history and recent archaeological evidence. There are seven stops along the way and at each one Basch shares its significance to the Puyallup. The tour takes you along the Prairie Line Trail, which was once part of the Northern Pacific Railroad. It contains artwork and interpretive signs throughout. It is interesting how the history of the town represents such a short period of time compared to that of the native peoples.

17th St. and Pacific Ave.
geotourist.com/tours/4419

EXPLORE
FARRELL MARSH

This is a true hidden treasure that is barely known outside Steilacoom. Town volunteers keep the trails in shape. The Chambers Street entrance has parking and a picnic table, which was an Eagle Scout project. There is also a posted map. Hike to the "Big Tree," which is the landmark you can use to find your way back if you lose your bearings. The trails rival those in the Olympic National Park rain forest with lush moss-covered trees and green ferns. The park has three viewpoints overlooking the freshwater shoreline of the marsh. Keep an eye out for blue herons and kingfishers and other waterfowl. The bridge takes you next to an impressive beaver dam and gives you another view of the marsh. Keep an eye out for small, laminated signs with poems, sayings, and information about the foliage. You may even see wagon ruts that were carved into the land 150 years ago.

Chambers St. and Beech Ave., Steilacoom
townofsteilacoom.org/258/farrells-marsh

EXPLORE THE BEAUTY
OF CHAMBERS CREEK REGIONAL PARK

This beautiful waterfront park has it all. Saltwater shoreline, urban creek and canyon, epic views of mountains and Puget Sound all vie for your attention. It wasn't always so lovely. The 930-acre park was once a sand and gravel mine. Legacy structures form iconic backdrops to the natural surroundings. The highlight of the park is its many trails, most of which are paved. Park at the bottom and take the Loop Trail, which combines the Grandview and the Soundview trails. You want to do the strenuous hike up the trail to the bluff first. It is not too bad after that, as you walk along the bluff, down a hill at the other end, and then loop back to the parking lot. There is a bridge that crosses over the railroad tracks to the beach. From it you can see Ketron, Anderson, McNeil, and Fox Islands. Keep an eye out for orcas, which occasionally visit this area. On a nice day, the beach is pleasant to stroll.

4800–4850 Grandview Dr. W, University Place, 253-798-4141
piercecountywa.gov/1317/chambers-creek-regional-park
chamberscreekfoundation.org/trails

GO SEE SOME SNOW
AT CRYSTAL MOUNTAIN RESORT

We have a saying, "Live like the Mountain is Out" based on the idea that if you can see Mount Rainier, then it is a gorgeous day to get outside. Crystal Mountain Resort offers fun outdoor activities both summer and winter. Take a ride on the Mount Rainier Gondola up 2,400 vertical feet to experience breathtaking views of Mount Rainier and more-distant mountains of the Cascades. Even during summer months there is snow on the mountain. In warmer months, discover the natural beauty of the Cascade Range by hiking the ridgelines and witnessing nature waking up after months of hibernation. In the winter months, hit the slopes. Crystal Mountain offers lessons and rentals with everything you need for a day of skiing or snowboarding. Snowshoeing is a great way to explore the winter scenery on foot with a professional guide. After spending time on the mountain, visit the Summit House, Washington's highest elevation restaurant. At 6,872 feet, you'll dine with gorgeous views of Mount Rainier. Menu changes seasonally.

33914 Crystal Mountain Blvd., Enumclaw, 833-279-7895
crystalmountainresort.com

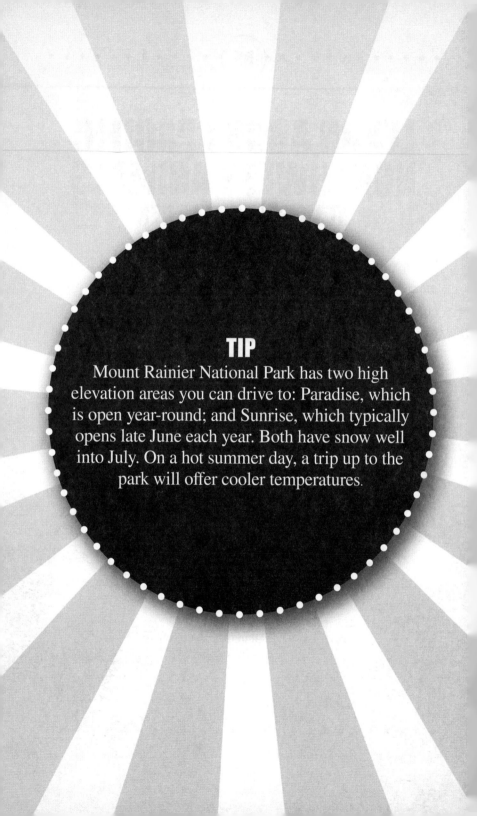

TIP

Mount Rainier National Park has two high elevation areas you can drive to: Paradise, which is open year-round; and Sunrise, which typically opens late June each year. Both have snow well into July. On a hot summer day, a trip up to the park will offer cooler temperatures.

LEARN ABOUT PACIFIC NORTHWEST ANIMALS
AT NORTHWEST TREK

Northwest Trek Wildlife Park is not your typical zoo, as it offers many opportunities to get up close with Pacific Northwest animals in their natural habitat. The Free-Roaming Area is home to herds of Roosevelt elk, bison, moose, caribou, bighorn sheep, mountain goats, swan, and deer on 435 acres that includes forest, meadow, and a lake. The park offers a variety of tours to experience this area. Eagle Passage will have visitors marveling at bald eagles in a habitat that includes old-growth Douglas firs. These eagles were injured and can't survive in the wild. If you luck out, you may see a bald eagle in the wild flying around the exhibit with the eagles "talking" to each other. Children will love the Kids' Trek playground with its Pacific Northwest theme. Such a fun unique playground made to resemble the forest. Take a stroll on the Animal Walking Paths to observe grizzlies, cougars, and more. Keep an eye out, as they can be anywhere in their large habitats.

11610 Trek Dr. E, Eatonville, 360-832-6117
nwtrek.org

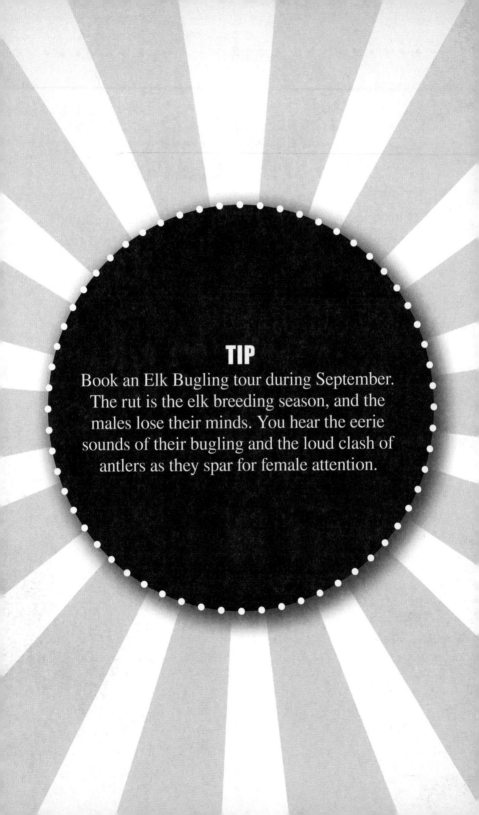

TIP

Book an Elk Bugling tour during September. The rut is the elk breeding season, and the males lose their minds. You hear the eerie sounds of their bugling and the loud clash of antlers as they spar for female attention.

DISCOVER
FORT STEILACOOM PARK

This historic site was used by the Nisqually and Steilacoom Indian tribes as a gathering place and source for food before fur traders and settlers moved into the area. It also served as a military fort before becoming Western State Hospital and a farm maintained by the patients. Historic buildings from the fort remain. The park is full of amenities and boasts over one million visitors annually. Outdoor enthusiasts will love the extensive trail system. The Discovery Trail offers a one-mile walk on a paved path around Waughop Lake. Other amenities include picnic shelters, restrooms, an off-leash dog park, and fields for soccer, baseball, and softball. The playground is arguably the best in Pierce County. Children will love this large, fortlike structure. This is a very active park, with walkers, runners, and dog walkers seen throughout the day. On weekends, multiple sporting events take place rain or shine. During the summer months there is a large, evening farmers market.

8714 87th Ave. SW, Lakewood, 253-983-7887
cityoflakewood.us/fort-steilacoom-park/

TIP

Across the street from the park is the
historic Fort Steilacoom Museum, which is
open only on the first Sunday of the month and
for special events. Well worth a visit to learn
more about the interesting history of this fort
established in 1849.

9601 Steilacoom Blvd., SW, Lakewood
historicfortsteilacoom.org/
info@historicfortsteilacoom.org

GO FOREST BATHING
IN MCCORMICK FOREST PARK

This lovely, wooded park is located right in Gig Harbor, but it feels miles away. The park has more than four miles of hiking and biking trails that are dog friendly. One route goes through the more than 50 acres of old-growth Douglas fir, which makes for a special experience. Shinrin-yoku, meaning "Forest Bathing," is becoming more popular as a way to increase the benefits of your walk while you explore the McCormick Forest. While walking in a forest, you encounter phytoncides, or essential oils, in the trees that are beneficial to your body. Wander with childlike wonder and take a few minutes to meditate while you breathe in the refreshing air scented with evergreen. You'll come out of the forest feeling relaxed and refreshed. Enjoy views of McCormick Creek and marvel at McCormick Creek Canyon. The trails are relatively flat, with just 200 feet of elevation gain, making it a perfect family hike.

10301 Bujacich Rd. NW, Gig Harbor, 253-858-3400
penmetparks.org/parks/mccormick-forest-park/

PICK SOME BLUEBERRIES
AT CHARLOTTE'S BLUEBERRY PARK

This is one of the more unique urban parks you will find. The site has been farmed since 1929. From 1952 until 1968 it was the Berg's Blueberry Farm. An active neighborhood group opposed the building of a school or other development of the property, which eventually was owned by Metro Parks Tacoma. Over the years the site became overgrown with unwanted vegetation, but the active neighborhood group wrote grants, volunteered, and saved the blueberry plants. Today, there are more than 3,372 bushes and 5 varieties of blueberries. During picking season, July–September, you can freely pick fresh blueberries that do not have any pesticides or fertilizers on the plants. Washington blueberries are so plump and tasty. Bring your own basket or bag to collect them. The park is 20 acres with 10 acres of wetlands. There is also a playground for children that overlooks the blueberry rows.

7402 E D St., 253-305-1000
metroparkstacoma.org/place/charlottes-blueberry-park/

BEACHCOMB
ALONG PUGET SOUND

Tacoma is a waterfront city and there are plenty of parks at which to enjoy a day at the beach. The land Titlow Park and Lodge sits on was used by the Puyallup and Nisqually Indians as a campsite. In its heyday around 1911, the lodge was the Hotel Hesperides, where guests came to enjoy the views of the Olympic Mountains, Fox Island, and Puget Sound. Today, visitors enjoy the extensive beach frontage and an estuary lagoon, which can be explored on two miles of trails. There are plenty of amenities with a sprayground, playground, picnic areas, and plenty of places for various sports activities. The sandy shoreline is a perfect venue for kayaking or paddleboarding. In the quaint town of Steilacoom, you will find Sunnyside Beach, which is popular with scuba divers and snorkelers because it is away from the strong narrows current and because of the marine life found there. The beachfront park also has a nice playground and plenty of picnic tables.

Titlow Park & Lodge
8425 6th Ave., 253-305-1000
metroparkstacoma.org/place/titlow-park-lodge/

Sunnyside Beach
Chambers Creek Rd., 253-581-1912
townofsteilacoom.org/264/Sunnyside-Beach

TEST YOUR MOUNTAIN BIKING SKILLS
AT SWAN CREEK PARK

Metro Parks Tacoma in partnership with the Evergreen Mountain Bike Alliance created an extensive 50-acre mountain bike trail network at Swan Creek Park. Beginners can try the easy perimeter trail and the technical skill-building zone, while more skilled riders will enjoy the advanced trails. The trails are in the uplands area of the park and non-motorized bikes can also access the paved trails in the area. Swan Creek Park is a beautiful natural area, which non-riders will enjoy as well. There is a salmon-bearing stream that flows through the park and wooded canyon. There are plenty of hiking trails throughout the park, which is popular for bird watching. One section of the park recently went through a $4 million upgrade. Highlights include a massive four acre off-leash dog park. Rather than a traditional playground, there is a new "pause and play" pathway that utilizes natural materials like tree stumps to create elements that spark the imagination and invite exploration.

3997 E Roosevelt Ave., 253-305-1000
metroparkstacoma.org/place/swan-creek-park/

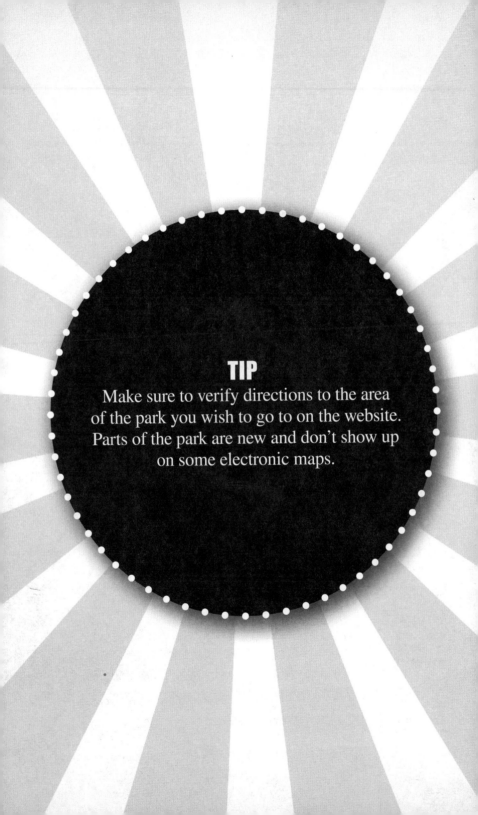

TIP

Make sure to verify directions to the area of the park you wish to go to on the website. Parts of the park are new and don't show up on some electronic maps.

CULTURE
AND HISTORY

WONDER AT MOLTEN GLASS
AT THE MUSEUM OF GLASS

As its name suggests, the Museum of Glass (MOG) is dedicated to showcasing works of art created out of glass. It is a very challenging medium to work with. There are live glass demonstrations each day the museum is open. The Hot Shop Team collaborates with visiting artists to bring to life the creative processes and techniques involved in creating a sculpture from molten glass. Tacoma native Dale Chihuly is known worldwide for his expressive glass art. The Spotlight on Dale Chihuly exhibition is in the museum's permanent collection and showcases examples of the various stages of his work. A highlight is the Gibson Chandelier, a visually stunning work of art. Art Deco aficionados will delight in almost 200 pieces of Rene Lalique's artwork from the Steven and Roslyn Shulman Collection. For a truly unique souvenir, visit the museum shop, where you can purchase a one-of-a-kind item designed and created in the MOG's Hot Shop and signed by the team.

1801 Dock St., 253-284-4750
museumofglass.org

MAKE SOME ART
AT THE TACOMA ART MUSEUM

The Tacoma Art Museum (TAM) focuses on the art and artists of the Northwest. The permanent collection of over 5,000 artworks, including works by Tacoma native Dale Chihuly. Families will enjoy the TAM Studio in the museum's lobby. No museum admission required. Inspired by the works of art in the TAM's collection, the hands-on activities are sure to inspire your budding artists. The studio is stocked with art supplies and lots of fun things to do. Check out the current "Invitation to Create," which includes ideas and the materials needed to create a project. Readers will love the complete collection of Caldecott Medal–winning picture books to be enjoyed in the Betty Gene and John Walker Reading Alcove.

1701 Pacific Ave., 253-272-4258
tacomaartmuseum.org

WALK THROUGH TIME
AT THE WASHINGTON STATE HISTORY MUSEUM

This huge museum is filled with so many fascinating interactive exhibits that children of all ages will enjoy. The Great Hall of Washington History—A Window to the Past is the largest exhibit in the museum. Learn about ancient peoples and Native cultures as well as the early settlers. The large dioramas and hands-on activities will keep your group busy for at least two hours. Make sure to check out the two new galleries that opened in 2021. Remembrance: The Legacy of Executive Order 9066 in Washington State is an exhibit about the Japanese American internment during World War II, which began not far from Tacoma on Bainbridge Island. The other new exhibit is 360, which refers to the 360-mile expanse of the state that runs from the sea to across the Cascades. This unique geography has abundant resources that attracted peoples to establish communities. Check out Anthem Coffee in the museum for a cup of joe or sandwiches.

1911 Pacific Ave., 253-272-3500
washingtonhistory.org

DISCOVER
THE BUFFALO SOLDIERS MUSEUM

This hidden gem of a museum was founded by William Jones and his family to preserve the memory of his time as a Buffalo Soldier during World War II (WWII). It is not often that a museum has such a personal connection. Located in a small house, the collection has an intimate feel to it. Jackie Jones-Hook, Jones's daughter, opened the museum in 2012, and it is one of only two museums in the United States dedicated to honoring the Buffalo Soldiers. It covers the history of the Buffalo Soldier from slavery and the Civil War to the integration of the Armed Forces. Although small, it packs in a lot that is forgotten in school textbooks. The museum is a labor of love and contains many artifacts from Jones's service to the military. In addition to serving during WWII, he was a prisoner of war during the Korean War.

1940 S Wilkeson St., 253-272-4257
buffalosoldierstacoma.org

GET AWESTRUCK
ON THE CHIHULY BRIDGE OF GLASS

The Chihuly Bridge of Glass is a stunning public work of art that consists of three distinct installations—the Seaform Pavilion, the Crystal Towers, and the Venetian Wall—created by Tacoma native Dale Chihuly. It is a pedestrian bridge that links the Foss Waterway and the Museum of Glass to Tacoma. From the Museum of Glass, you will come to the Venetian Wall, which displays 109 glass sculptures by Chihuly. The 80-foot-long wall contains some of the largest glass pieces ever blown. Next up are the Crystal Towers, which are massive translucent blue structures created from glass. The inspiration was the glacial, blue ice found at Mount Rainier. These make for an iconic Tacoma image that appears different in the changing light. They form a beacon when illuminated at night. The Seaform Pavilion is so named due to the over 2,000 objects in its ceiling that create the illusion of being underwater. The Museum of Glass offers a walking tour of the Bridge of Glass and the Thea Foss Waterway.

Bridge of Glass, Tacoma
museumofglass.org/tours

REFLECT ON MISTAKES OF THE PAST
AT THE TACOMA CHINESE RECONCILIATION PARK

This lovely park serves as a reminder of the shameful past when a large group of men physically expelled the Chinese people from Tacoma. In the days that followed, townspeople destroyed their homes and businesses. Located on Ruston Way, the park is intended as a place of healing and harmony, and you do have a sense of peace as you walk through this tranquil garden located near the site of the early Chinese settlement called Little Canton. To explore the park, begin at the entrance by the large sign and read about this history. Then follow the interpretive path through the Chinese garden while taking in the natural beauty of Commencement Bay. There are a variety of exhibits and artworks along the way. The park is part of the Ruston Way Waterfront, which is a series of parks connected by a paved path. There is public parking all along the way. Arrive early, as it is very popular.

1741 N Schuster Pkwy., 253-330-8828
tacomachinesepark.org

IMMERSE YOURSELF IN MARITIME HISTORY
AT THE FOSS WATERWAY SEAPORT

This heritage museum is a hands-on way to explore the rich, maritime history of Tacoma and Puget Sound. The museum building is the last remaining section of what was once the longest wheat warehouse in the world. It has been restored and serves as a museum, a boat shop, and an education facility. It even has dock moorage. The Rails Met Sails exhibit brings to life the history of the western terminus for the Northern Pacific Railroad. The scale model of the Tacoma Wharf with running trains is fascinating. Located on traditional Puyallup land, this exhibit seeks to share the rich culture and heritage of the Puyallup people. The active heritage wooden boat shop works to preserve the techniques and craftsmanship of regional boat builders. Make sure to take some time and explore the dock area and the great views of the area.

705 Dock St., 253-272-2750
fosswaterwayseaport.org

EXPLORE
A NEIGHBORHOOD BUSINESS DISTRICT

When driving around Tacoma you will often stumble upon vibrant neighborhood businesses. These mini–Main Streets add to a small town feeling amid the larger city of Tacoma. There are 15 of these districts and each has its own unique vibe. Many are also historic districts as well. The website gives you an overview of each district and allows you to download a brochure that profiles the highlights. This is where you will find the places locals frequent, the shops and restaurants in their own neighborhoods. The Lincoln International Business District recently underwent a revitalization project that created sidewalk improvements as well as an Asian-themed entryway and streetlamps. The Asian shops and restaurants are authentic and unique. The 14 other districts each have their own distinctive flair and provide a great way to discover the cultures that make up Tacoma.

tacomabusinessdistricts.com/district-profiles/

JUMP BACK IN TIME
AT THE FORT NISQUALLY LIVING HISTORY MUSEUM

If you ever wanted to know what it was like to reside near Puget Sound in 1855, then visit the Fort Nisqually Living History Museum located in Point Defiance. This is a 1930s reconstruction of the original fort, which was in Dupont and was the first European settlement on Puget Sound, built by the Hudson Bay Company. Volunteers and staff dress in period clothing and demonstrate the work, crafts, and social practices of the times. There are seven buildings. Two of the structures, the Factor's House and Granary, are historical structures preserved and donated by local citizens. All the buildings are historically furnished. The Heritage Gardens offer a unique insight into the history of the fort and reflect 19th-century agricultural practices. Great effort goes into this, including the discovery at a seed bank of a type of wheat grown by the Hudson Bay Company. There are apple trees grafted from the trees at the original Fort Nisqually site.

5519 Five Mile Dr., 253-404-3970
metroparkstacoma.org/place/fort-nisqually-living-history-museum/

TIP

Hike the Sequalitchew Creek Trail in Dupont, which will give you a feel for the original site of Fort Nisqually.

LEARN ABOUT MILITARY HISTORY
AT THE LEWIS ARMY MUSEUM

When driving south on I-5, you can't help but notice the striking white building just past Exit 120. This is the Lewis Army Museum, one of the few buildings on the base dating back to World War I. It is also the only building from Greene Park, which was a recreational area for soldiers stationed at what was then Camp Lewis. It was constructed for the Salvation Army as a Red Shield Inn and in later years became a hotel for soldiers and their families before becoming the Lewis Army Museum. The museum has state-of-the-art exhibits that trace the military history of the base and the units stationed here to the present day. Keep an eye out among the exhibits for a female Asian American soldier with the name Flint, the adopted daughter of the museum director, Erik Flint. There is also a great gift shop with military-themed items and toys for children.

4320 Main St. and Constitution Dr., Joint Base Lewis–McChord
253-967-7206
lewisarmymuseum.com

TIP

At Milepost 120 off I-5, stop to see the Captain Meriwether Lewis Monument, the namesake of Fort Lewis and commander of the Corps of Discovery. Also at this site is the iconic Liberty Gate, which was built and paid for by workers who constructed the original Camp Lewis.

DISCOVER WHAT LIFE WAS LIKE
IN A COMPANY TOWN AT THE DUPONT HISTORICAL MUSEUM

This darling little museum shares the history of Dupont through four eras beginning with that of the Native Americans who originally settled this area. The Hudson Bay Company and the original Fort Nisqually were the first European settlers here. They are featured second. Next, exhibits depict what life was like working for the Dupont Company and living in the town. Finally, there is information on the Weyerhaeuser's planned community, Northwest Landing. The historic Dupont Company town still exists, and you can download the walking tour from the museum's website. It is tucked away, and many people don't know its unique history. Old Dupont is undergoing a renaissance, and the old company cottages are highly sought real estate.

207 Barksdale Ave., DuPont, 253-964-2399
dupontmuseum.com

TIP

Grab picnic fixings from Mince Mercantile, a cute petite grocery store in New Dupont. Every day, there are freshly prepared breakfast and lunch offerings.

1495 Wilmington Dr., DuPont
253-302-5331

DISCOVER CHIHULY
AT UNION STATION

A stop at Union Station is a must when visiting downtown Tacoma. Superstar famed glass artist Dale Chihuly was born and raised in the gritty city. He has generously donated public works of art to various venues around town. His works shown at Union Station were created specifically for the site and beautifully enhance the historic train station. Built in 1911, the domed Union Station was designed by Reed & Stem, the architects acclaimed for New York's Grand Central Station. The Romanesque Revival style of the building makes the perfect backdrop for Chihuly's work. One of his signature chandeliers hangs in the rotunda and is stunning. Although you can see all the works from the first floor, take a moment to walk upstairs and observe them up close. Best of all, the entire experience is free and conveniently located next to the Tacoma Art Museum and the Washington History Museum.

1717 Pacific Ave., 253-863-5173
traveltacoma.com/listings/union-station/198/

BECOME AN HONORARY LIGHTKEEPER
AT BROWNS POINT LIGHTHOUSE PARK

This darling park has a small, recently restored lighthouse and a 1903 historic lighthouse keeper's cottage that you can rent. The accommodations require a "tour of duty," where you raise and lower the flag and log in the weather and shipping traffic. Saturdays add the additional duties of opening the Cottage and Museum for visitors. What a fun experience for families. It is located at the tip of historic Browns Point on the shores of Puget Sound. Enjoy walking the beach, fishing, and taking in the epic sunsets. The park has plenty of green space and is a perfect site for day visitors to enjoy a picnic. Visitors enjoy watching ships enter the Port of Tacoma or sailboats on nice days. To get here, you drive through the Browns Point Neighborhood with its beautiful old homes. This park is tucked away but well worth the effort to find.

201 Tulalip St. NE, 253-927-2536
pointsnorthwest.org/cottage-rental

STAY IN A TUDOR GOTHIC CASTLE
AT THORNEWOOD CASTLE

Known as the "house that love built," this home was built by Chester Thorne for his wife Anna. He purchased a 400-year-old Elizabethan manor and had it shipped to the Pacific Northwest. Renowned architect Kirtland Kelsey Cutter, famed for the iconic Liberty Gate at Fort Lewis, was the architect. This stunning building contains over 100 pieces of stained glass salvaged from 15th- and 16th-century churches. The original property is now a gated community, and the only way to experience this historic building is to book lodging. During your stay, enjoy the lovely common areas, which include a game room, a library, a movie room, and a stunning Great Hall and summer porch with a lake view. Outside, explore three acres of grounds and the beautiful sunken English garden designed by the Olmsted brothers, sons of Frederick Law Olmstead, who designed Central Park in New York City.

8601 N Thorne Ln. SW, Lakewood, 253-584-4393
thornewoodcastle.com

TOUR THE ART COLLECTION
AT THE STUNNING HOTEL MURANO

You know that a hotel named after Murano, Italy—famed as the Old-World capital of glass art—is going to have an incredible glass art collection. Tacoma is an epicenter of American glass art, which is the theme for the hotel. The collection includes a carefully curated collection that includes pieces specifically created for sites within the hotel and acquisitions from artists. Twelve countries and 45 artists are represented throughout the hotel. It is an eclectic collection of various art techniques and styles. Keep an eye out for Dale Chihuly's work in the lobby. It truly is museum worthy. You don't have to be a guest at the hotel to enjoy the collection. Take a docent-led tour of the hotel, which will let you appreciate this beautiful collection. To schedule, contact the hotel at info@hotelmuranotacoma.com.

1310 Broadway, 253-238-8000
provenancehotels.com/hotel-murano-tacoma

IMMERSE IN HISTORY
AT THE JOB CARR CABIN MUSEUM AT OLD TOWN PARK

Job Carr was Tacoma's first non-Native resident, and a replica of his frontier cabin sits at Old Town Park. Docent-led tours share stories of Job Carr and old Tacoma taken from the family diaries and other historic sources. Period furnishings and interiors add to the historic ambiance. Carr is one of Tacoma's founding fathers, and his life is one of firsts. His cabin served as Tacoma's first post office and the location of its first election. He served on the first city council and became the first mayor of Tacoma. The park is near the area known as Old Town Tacoma. Walk down 30th Street on the sidewalks and take note of the plaques embedded in the sidewalks, which commemorate significant achievements of notable Tacoma women.

2350 N 30th St., 253-305-1000
metroparkstacoma.org/place/old-town-park/

LEARN THE LEGEND OF GALLOPING GERTIE
AT THE HARBOR HISTORY MUSEUM

There is a lot of museum packed in this small place, but every inch is used wisely. The main gallery is stuffed with exhibits on the rich heritage of the Gig Harbor Peninsula. Many are interactive with videos, hands-on displays, or computer exhibits that visitors of all ages will enjoy. The Tacoma Narrows Bridge, which you crossed to get to Gig Harbor, has an infamous past as "Galloping Gertie." The original bridge collapsed in 1940 after buckling and galloping in the high winds. Remnants of the bridge became a reef. Legend has it a giant octopus lives there. Harbor History Museum has an interesting exhibit devoted to Gertie, and you can see video footage of the bridge before it collapsed. During your visit, make sure to go outside to see the restored Midway Schoolhouse and the museum galleries. Experience school at the turn of the century. The Shenandoah, a 65-foot purse seiner, was built in 1925 and donated to the museum. It is currently being restored, and you can talk to the volunteers about the process.

4121 Harborview Dr., Gig Harbor, 253-858-6722
harborhistorymuseum.org/

BE INTRIGUED
AT THE KARPELES
MANUSCRIPT MUSEUM

There are 17 of these unique museums around the United States, each in a small- to medium-sized city and housed in a historical building. David and Marsha Karpeles began the museums to share their collection, the largest in the world, of more than one million historic manuscripts and documents. The goal was to stimulate interest in learning among children. The Tacoma museum is located across from Wright Park in the former American Legion Post built in 1931. It is free to the public and showcases a variety from the collection, which is rotated among the 17 museums. There is a new exhibit every three months. Exhibits are displayed in oak and glass cases, and there is such a variety. Highlights include The Bill of Rights, Darwin's The Theory of Evolution, and Richard Wagner's "Wedding March." Papers from famous historical figures come from Amelia Earhart, George Washington, Che Guevara, Mark Twain, and so many more.

407 S G St., 253-383-2575
karpeles.com/museums/taq.php

BE ENTHRALLED
WITH THE RARE PLANTS AT THE W.W. SEYMOUR BOTANICAL CONSERVATORY

Located in Wright Park, a 27-acre arboretum and public park, the W.W. Seymour Botanical Conservatory is a Tacoma treasure. It is one of only three public Victorian-style conservatories on the West Coast and is on the National Historic register. It opened in 1908 through a generous gift from its namesake. For more than 100 years it has enthralled city residents with its tropical, rare, and exotic plants. In an area where the weather is gray and damp during the winter months, the conservatory provided a warm and beautiful venue with bright colors to dispel the winter blues. The current collection contains ferns, palms, figs, bromeliads, orchids, and many other rate plants. Throughout the year there are floral exhibits and other events. The conservatory gift shop sells plants and other garden-themed merchandise and jewelry. After touring the conservatory, spend some time walking through Wright Park and its over 700 mature trees.

316 S G St., 253-404-3975
metroparkstacoma.org/place/w-w-seymour-conservatory/

VISIT THE STEILACOOM
HISTORICAL MUSEUM

Lovely Steilacoom is a city of firsts. It is the first incorporated town in Washington, had the first school district, the first library, the first jail, the first post office, among many more firsts. The main museum building is tiny but packs quite a bit of history in the small space, with so many interesting exhibits. The museum complex also includes two historical buildings, the Nathaniel Orr Home and Orchard, built in 1852, and the Wagon Shop, built in 1870. Volunteer docents are available to answer any questions. The museum has limited hours, but you can still view the sites on a historic walking tour that you can download from the historical society website. The Bair Bistro leases the Bair Drug and Hardware Store, which belongs to the historical society. Step back in time as you enter this living history museum with the walls and shelves lined with relics and photos. Grab a table, order a soda from the original 1908 soda fountain, and enjoy fresh, made-to-order entrées.

1801 Rainier St., Steilacoom, 253-584-4133
steilacoomhistorical.org
steilacoomhistorical.org/steilacoom_walking_tour.pdf

SHOPPING
AND FASHION

SHOP TILL YOU DROP
AT PINE AND MOSS

This darling shop is a dream come true for owner Kimberlee Cavin, a retired military spouse. It is not only a store but a community. Kimberlee knows the challenges military spouses face in finding employment, so she tries to hire them. She also sources locally as much as possible from artists and purveyors around the Pacific Northwest. Pine and Moss is a go-to shop for gifts, and with local food artisans (products so good they should be called art) like Seattle Chocolates and Coro Foods (handcrafted charcuterie) you can find gourmet additions to up your picnic game. There is an eclectic mix of children's toys, clothing, skin care products, and home décor. There truly is something for everyone. Cavin combines her southern heritage with the Pacific Northwest spirit to create a unique shop inspired by tradition with a modern flair.

1100 Station Dr., Suite 141, DuPont, 253-302-5071
shoppineandmoss.com

DISCOVER FEEL-GOOD FASHION
AT 27 WEST

Stephanie Curnow is a busy mom, military spouse, and entrepreneur, and 27 West is one result of her hard work. You won't find stuffy, uncomfortable clothing at 27 West but rather pieces that make you look and feel good. Curnow personally curates each piece with an eye to helping busy moms look pulled together while keeping prices affordable. She has set her business model with goals, the first being to provide quality clothing and great customer service at affordable prices. The second is to provide employment opportunities for military spouses, whose unemployment rate is 16 percent, four times the national average. So, shop small, where your purchase can make a difference and there are cute clothes.

1430 Wilmington Dr., Suite 160, Dupont, 253-293-5806
shop27west.com

EXPLORE KOREAN SHOPPING
AT SHIN SHIN

Shin Shin is a Korean home goods store filled with all kinds of unique treasures. Korean skincare has seen a surge in popularity, especially the paper facemasks, which are a steal here. Children will love the training chopsticks. Although Shin Shin primarily features home goods, make sure to go down every aisle, as you never know what you will find. There are lots of Korean herbal remedies, like ginseng. Also take time to watch the videos demonstrating Korean kitchen appliances. So interesting. Be prepared for excellent customer service, which can be a little intimidating if you aren't used to the culture. The salespeople are not following you because they think you are stealing but to help you with your selections and to make suggestions. Truly a fun adventure and a cultural experience.

8726 S Tacoma Way, 253-582-2975
facebook.com/shin-shin-185403424809526

WANDER
WATSON'S GREENHOUSE AND NURSERY

Visiting a greenhouse and nursery in a travel guide? Absolutely! In addition to gardening, Watson's has a 32,500-square-foot glass and steel greenhouse from Belgium that is stunning. Shop the extended line of gifts and garden art as well as gardening products and plants. Watson's grows most of their annuals and makes their own containers and hanging planters. Take the time to walk the rows and view all the beautiful plants, especially in spring and summer. The designers are pros and they put together some gorgeous containers with unique plant combinations. Perfect for a hostess gift when visiting friends or family. After you work up an appetite, visit the on-site Fran's Garden Bistro. With its cute "ladies who lunch" vibe, it is a fun place to eat. The menu offers, paninis, sandwiches, soups, salads, and quiche. The soups are house-made daily, and the bistro offers daily specials.

6211 Pioneer Way E, Puyallup, 253-845-7359
shop.watsonsgreenhouse.com

DON'T GET LOST
AT FREIGHTHOUSE SQUARE

What an eclectic experience it is exploring Freighthouse Square! This plucky group of entrepreneurs run a variety of businesses, many of them minority owned, in an iconic historic building that continues to reinvent itself. Built around 1910, it was once the Milwaukee–St. Paul Railroad Station, and Freighthouse and now has a faded vintage feel to it that is part of its charm. The businesses come and go, so you never know what you will find, but it is sure to be interesting. The building is huge, spanning three blocks at five stories tall. It houses everything from antique shops, art galleries, kitschy shops, and even an escape room. The food court has a local cult following, and you will find an international mix of food choices there. Make sure to visit the Olive Branch Café, which is decorated with reclaimed items. It is beautifully historic looking and offers lunch and tea. Free parking is avilable across the street in the parking garage. It is at the Tacoma Dome Station, where you can catch the Link light rail, which will take you downtown.

2501 E D St., 253-305-0678

TIP

On the corner opposite Freighthouse Square you will see a warehouse building and a yellow door, the entrance to Johnny's Fine Foods. This iconic local brand has been around for over 70 years, and the seasoning salt of choice for area chefs is Johnny's. It is their top-selling product, and while you can find it in local stores, it is a fun experience going through the yellow door, into the office to purchase Johnny's products.

SHOP LOCAL
AT THE POINT RUSTON PUBLIC MARKET

The Point Ruston Public Market is located in the waterfront resort village of Point Ruston, with its incredible panoramic views of Puget Sound and the Olympic Mountains. The market is an eclectic mix of permanent tenants and, on weekends, non-permanent day-stall vendors. You'll find local produce, a full-service butcher, and flower vendors. Where the market shines is with the local artisans and purveyors who ply their wares, including bath and body products, olive oil, and specialty foods. Make sure to stop at Taco Street, a family-owned business that, as the name implies, makes some seriously good street tacos. They have lots of options, including family packs. On a nice day, head outside to the patio to enjoy your meal with the great views Point Ruston is known for.

5101 Yacht Club Rd., Ruston, 253-752-2185
pointruston.com/public_market

VISIT UPTOWN GIG HARBOR
FOR UPSCALE SHOPPING

This is upscale-boutique shopping at its finest. Vibrant Uptown Gig Harbor's mission is to make shopping fun again, and they do, with an outdoor shopping center designed like a town plaza. The vibe here is relaxed and friendly. Grab a cup of coffee and stroll the Art Walk that takes you through the landscaped grounds where you can experience all types of art from contemporary sculpture to traditional gongs. Shoppers will love the 35 chic retailers that are a mix of national chains and local merchants. For entertainment, enjoy one of the many restaurants from quick takeout to fine dining. Watch a movie at the Galaxy Theater and IMAX. Before visiting, make sure to view the website for fun events such as performances by local school bands or individual store events like "sip and shop." Also look for specials. There is always something on sale.

4701 Point Fosdick Dr., Gig Harbor, 253-851-4557
uptowngigharbor.com

SUPPORT A COLLECTION
OF LOCAL, FAMILY-OWNED BUSINESSES

Local mother–daughter team Jennifer Luna and her mom Laurie Hicks have earned a cult following for their collection of small retail businesses located near each other in Fircrest. They began with Paper Luxe Stationery and Gifts, where you can find all kinds of gifts and cards. The Pacific Northwest section has a great selection of locally themed items perfect for souvenirs of the area. Due to the success of their children's line, they opened the Curious Bear Toy and Book Shop next door. The COVID-19 pandemic created a demand for gifts and goods for the home, so they opened The Crest Home. Two additional stores are now in Gig Harbor. They have also started their own online greeting card venture, Kindship Cards, which celebrates independent greeting card artists. The business provides the opportunity to discover new artists while knowing your dollars are spent with a purpose. A percentage of each order supports charitable organizations.

Paper Luxe Stationery and Gifts
2053 Mildred St. W, Fircrest, 253-328-4967
paper-luxe.com

The Crest Home
2057 Mildred St. W, Fircrest, 253-201-7171
thecresthome.com

The Curious Bear Toy and Book Shop
2061 Mildred St. W, Fircrest, 253-328-7192
curiousbeartoys.com

Paper Luxe Stationery and Gifts
4729 Point Fosdick Dr., Suite 300, Gig Harbor,
253-900-2132
paper-luxe.com

Little Luxe Baby
4729 Point Fosdick Dr., Suite 100, Gig Harbor,
253-900-2244
littleluxebaby.com

GIVE BACK
WITH A PURCHASE AT COMPASS ROSE TACOMA

Compass Rose donates 10 percent of their earnings to local charities that improve our community and international nonprofits working to alleviate poverty. The store, located in the charming, historic Proctor neighborhood, houses a thoughtfully curated collection of Pacific Northwest goods, handcrafted jewelry, paper goods, and home décor. The shop is light and colorful, which is important on gray Pacific Northwest days. The decorated displays are arranged to highlight the lovely offerings, each of which is carefully selected. Local is important as is sustainability in determining what is worthy to be in the store. If you need a gift, this is the place to go. When finished shopping, take some time to explore this walkable neighborhood filled with craftsman-style homes, darling shops, and eclectic restaurants.

3815 N 26th St., 253-759-0077
compassroseshop.com

POP IN TO TICKLED PINK
FOR FUN, INSPIRED SHOPPING

This cute shop is in "downtown" Gig Harbor. This is the area that surrounds the waterfront and is known for its local small businesses. It is a great walkable community with a Main Street program, where you will find fun events almost every month of the year. Tickled Pink is a big supporter of the community. You'll often find their gift cards in fundraisers for local schools, sports, and arts programs. Your shopping dollars contribute to Tickled Pink's donations to local nonprofits. The store is packed to the brim with an eclectic mix of products. You'll find Pacific Northwest–inspired items as well as specialty boutique brands. Tickled Pink is known for their scarves, which sell like hotcakes. Fashionable accessories such as hats and jewelry are all affordable. There is also a store at Point Ruston.

3026 Harborview Dr., Gig Harbor, 252-858-1751
tickledpinkstores.com

Tickled Pink Point Ruston
5060 Main St., 253-302-5097
tickledpinkstores.com

GET LOST EXPLORING
AT SANFORD AND SON ANTIQUES

Tacoma's Antique Row is made up of a diverse collection of shops and antique stores located in one of the most historic areas of downtown. The granddaddy of them all is the behemoth Sanford and Son Antiques. The store is so large you can enter on the ground floor on Broadway and exit a few stories up on Commerce Street. There are 3 floors and 25,000 square feet of antiques, books, oddities, and other treasures. It is the largest, singly owned antique shop in the Pacific Northwest. There is even a display with the lid of an Egyptian sarcophagus. The Middle Floor Merchants are 20 shops and services that are individually owned. You'll find thousands of books in the library, which is two-tiered and can be rented for events. Spend some time strolling Broadway and explore some of the other stores in the area. Truly a unique experience.

743 Broadway, 253-272-0334

CURE YOUR SWEET TOOTH
AT THE BROWN AND
HALEY FACTORY STORE

This iconic factory–store combo is a must stop when visiting Tacoma. You can't tour the over 100-year-old factory, but the outside is pretty cool, with its vintage charm and iconic neon light. In 1962, Brown and Haley purchased the ticket booth from the 1962 World's Fair, held in Seattle. Elvis Presley was in the building during the filming of *It Happened at the World's Fair*, where it was used as a green room for him between scenes. This tiny building is a candy lover's dream, with factory-outlet prices on Almond Roca and all the other Rocas, the company's famed concoction. Mountain Bars are another candy they are famed for. The signature gold-and-pink packaging filled with Almond Roca have been popular since 1923. In the 1990s, Almond Roca became the largest exported gift candy in the United States; it is shipped to 63 countries.

110 E 26th St., 253-620-3067
brown-haley.com

TREAT YOURSELF
AT JOHNSON CANDY COMPANY

The Johnson family has handcrafted chocolates since 1925 after surviving the early years of a very competitive market. Candy makers fell by the wayside, including Frank Mars, who later found success with the Mars Candy company in Minnesota. The Johnson Candy Company's success is due to great products that are made fresh daily by William Johnson and his father Ron, who still comes in daily. A top seller is the open-faced caramel with roasted California almonds dipped in milk or dark chocolate. The caramel is rich, buttery, and super soft, just firm enough to hold its shape. This is seriously good candy. The company is in the Hilltop neighborhood in its now-iconic building built in 1949. The Link light rail expansion travels right by the Johnson Candy Company.

924 M.L.K. Jr Way, 253-272-8504
johnsoncandyco.com

DISCOVER
PACIFIC NORTHWEST PRODUCTS

The Pacific Northwest Shop is a must stop for both locals and tourists. Locals love to shop here for unique gifts, while visitors can find the perfect souvenir of their trip. These aren't your made-in-China knickknacks with Tacoma stamped on them but a carefully curated selection of local products from around the Pacific Northwest. How unique is a glass Christmas ornament made from ash created when Mount St. Helens erupted? You'll find a great selection of candies, food products, and Washington wines. Regional artists who craft jewelry, pottery, and other artworks are featured. The store is nestled in the Proctor neighborhood, where you will find a variety of shops and restaurants that are easy to explore on foot. It is a fun neighborhood with a vibrant farmers market on Saturday mornings.

2702 N Proctor St., 253-752-2242
pacificnorthwestshop.com

LOSE YOURSELF AMONG THE SHELVES
AT THE TACOMA BOOK CENTER

There are over 180,000 books stacked floor to ceiling at the Tacoma Book Center. It is a Mecca for booklovers, who can get lost among the shelves browsing for hours. The company also runs an online business with an additional 300,000 books. Chances are they have that out-of-print treasure you are searching for. The staff is helpful and friendly with a good knowledge of people, offering help if you need it or knowing when you just want to browse. The center has a large children's section carrying many parents' own childhood favorites. This is not a modern bookstore; the books are used, and it is a maze of stock everywhere, but that is its charm. There is a sense of discovery as you wonder the shelves not knowing what you will find.

324 E 26th St., 253-572-8248

DISCOVER A VINTAGE TREASURE
AT D. HABERDASHERY

Dion Teague is known as the "Most Fashionable Man" in Tacoma. He curates a collection of men's vintage clothing for sale at his Broadway shop. You'll find dress shoes, in particular the classic leather oxford, Levi's, vintage hats, and watches. He is also a fan of Pendleton wool shirts, which pair so well with a pair of vintage Levi's. If you are ready to up your wardrobe game with classic clothes that won't break the bank, this is the place to go. Dion can help you craft a look that will give you your own unique style. These aren't your typical thrift shop finds but high-quality pieces that are very well made. He carries a variety of styles, and you may even luck out and find a Hawaiian shirt, the perfect attire for the tiki bar in McMenamin's Elk Temple.

748 Broadway, 253-241-7561

FIND YOUR NEXT READ
AT KING'S BOOKS

King's Books is an independent bookstore located in the Stadium Historic District in a century-old building just perfect for a bookstore. There are approximately 100,000 new and used books for sale. Owner sweet pea Flaherty has turned the place into a true community-oriented hangout that welcomes diversity. You'll find weekly events from community gatherings to author readings and book signings. Flaherty is a literary icon in Tacoma, and his events are very creative and hugely popular. The book clubs that meet at the store are an eclectic mix from the Classics Book Club to the Feminist Utopia Book Club and everything between. He has created a true community of booklovers and a great place to hang out. As you are shopping, keep an eye out for Herbert, the shop cat peeking around bookshelves or napping.

218 St. Helens Ave., 253-272-8801
kingsbookstore.com

SUPPORT LOCAL ARTISTS
AT THE 253 COLLECTIVE ART GALLERY

Founder Linda Danforth had a vision to create a retail space for local artists while keeping costs low. The 253 Collective was the answer. It is a cooperative in which each artist pays a small monthly membership fee and has a job within the collective, such as marketing or maintaining the gallery. Each artist also takes a day each month running the gallery. It is a win for these talented creators who receive full payment for their sold works, with no commission. Art lovers enjoy meeting local artists each time they shop, and you can gain insight into their works. The collective hosts events throughout the month. These can be receptions for new featured artists or the $50 and Below Show with a Last Chance Reception. If you want more information about the artists, you can find their profiles on the website.

1901 Jefferson Ave.
253collective.com

CRAFT A MASTERPIECE
AT TINKERTOPIA

Children and adults love coming in to Tinkertopia, where their imaginations can run wild. Founded by two Tacoma artists, Tinkertopia strives for planetary-resource conservation, more commonly known as "upcycling." They work with local industries to repurpose scraps, discards, and overstocks into low-cost arts-and-crafts supplies. The bonus is it helps the environment by removing these items from the waste stream. So many options. You can purchase bags of varying sizes and fill them with what you like from the amazing selection. Out of towners often find a unique "historic" souvenir, or you can book a 90-minute Tinker Time session to craft your own masterpiece. For the bargain price of $10 you can access the Tinker Space and all the supplies needed. It is such a fun and creative way to enjoy the Tacoma art scene. It's a great activity for after a museum visit.

1914 Pacific Ave., 253-778-6539
tinkertopia.com

FIND A TREASURE
AT TRICKY'S POP CULTURE EMPORIUM

Take time to pop into (pun intended) Tricky's Pop Culture Emporium for a truly distinctive shopping experience. Tricky, short for Patrick, is a local character who transformed his hoarding and collecting tendencies into a successful business. He sells pop culture wonders, collectibles, toys, T-shirts, and just plain junk. Tricky has the best inventory in Tacoma if you love pop culture. He has over 1,000 Barbies, thousands of Funko Pops, and just about every pop culture trend from Star Trek to Marvel. You never know what you'll find when you come in. The inventory is like a mini museum. Tricky has a knack for helping you find the perfect item, whether for yourself or for a gift. He stocks the store based on what he thinks is cool, which makes for a diverse mix, especially the action figures.

17 N Tacoma Ave., Tacoma, 253-272-5288
poptricky.com

ACTIVITIES
BY SEASON

WINTER

Go See Some Snow at Crystal Mountain Resort, 70

Find Your Inner Lumberjack at Bullseye Lane Axe Throwing, 48

Escape from Mayan Ruins at Escape Hour, 39

Find a Treasure at Hi-Voltage Records and Books, 49

Be Intrigued at the Karpeles Manuscript Museum, 106

Lose Yourself among the Shelves at the Tacoma Book Center, 128

Cure Your Sweet Tooth at the Brown and Haley Factory Store, 125

Tour the Art Collection at the Stunning Hotel Murano, 102

Be Enthralled with the Rare Plants at the W.W. Seymour Botanical Conservatory, 107

SPRING

Experience a Traditional Links Golf Course at Chambers Bay, 57

Explore Land and Sea at Point Defiance Zoo and Aquarium, 58

Reflect on Mistakes of the Past at the Tacoma Chinese Reconciliation Park, 89

Explore Farrell Marsh, 68

See More from Your Feet Than from Your Seat with a Tacoma Brewery Row Tour, 38

Wander Watson's Greenhouse and Nursery, 115

SUMMER

Pick Some Blueberries at Charlotte's Blueberry Park, 77
Hope for the Environment at Dune Peninsula Park, 66
Be Serenaded on the Gig Harbor Gondola, 32
Rent an Electric Bike to Explore Point Defiance Five Mile Drive, 63
Beachcomb Along Puget Sound, 78
Take Me Out to the Ball Game with the Tacoma Rainiers, 56
Sway to Live Music at the Steilacoom Farmers Market, 33

FALL

Become an Honorary Lightkeeper at Browns Point Lighthouse Park, 100
Explore Farrell Marsh, 68
Jump Back in Time at the Fort Nisqually Living History Museum, 92
Immerse in History at the Job Carr Cabin Museum at Old Town Park, 104
Learn about Pacific Northwest Animals at Northwest Trek, 72
Hike the Sequalitchew Creek Trail, 64
Discover What Life Was Like in a Company Town
    at the Dupont Historical Museum, 96

SUGGESTED
ITINERARIES

EXPLORE HISTORIC STEILACOOM

Sip a Cup of Joe in a Historic Setting at Topside Coffee Cabin, 8
Explore Farrell Marsh, 68
Sway to Live Music at the Steilacoom Farmers Market, 33
Visit the Steilacoom Historical Museum, 108
Beachcomb Along Puget Sound, 78

FAMILY FUN

Escape from Mayan Ruins at Escape Hour, 39
Pick Some Blueberries at Charlotte's Blueberry Park, 77
Jump Back in Time at the Fort Nisqually Living History Museum, 92
Learn about Pacific Northwest Animals at Northwest Trek, 72
Get Serious about Gaming at Ocean5, 40
Explore Land and Sea at Point Defiance Zoo and Aquarium, 58
Craft a Masterpiece at Tinkertopia, 132

DISCOVER DALE CHIHULY

Get Awestruck on the Chihuly Bridge of Glass, 88
Tour the Art Collection at the Stunning Hotel Murano, 102
Wonder at Molten Glass at the Museum of Glass, 84
Blow a Work of Art at the Tacoma Glass Studio, 45
Make Some Art at the Tacoma Art Museum, 85
Discover Chihuly at Union Station, 98

DATE NIGHT

Be Stunned by the Views at Copper & Salt Northwest Kitchen, 2
Slink Into the Speakeasy Vibe at El Gaucho, 4
Be Serenaded on the Gig Harbor Gondola, 32
Sing Along with Dueling Musicians at Keys on Main, 50
Chill Out to Live Music at the Spanish Ballroom, 34
Elevate Your Steakhouse Experience at Stanford's Steak, 11
Delight in the Sizzling Hot Stones at Cuerno Bravo, 13
Stay in a Tudor Gothic Castle at Thornewood Castle, 101

GET OUTSIDE

Take the Ferry to Explore Anderson Island, 59
Become an Honorary Lightkeeper at Browns Point Lighthouse Park, 100
Experience a Traditional Links Golf Course at Chambers Bay, 57
Explore the Beauty of Chambers Creek Regional Park, 69
Hope for the Environment at Dune Peninsula Park, 66
Explore Farrell Marsh, 68
Discover Fort Steilacoom Park, 74
Go Forest Bathing in McCormick Forest Park, 76
Hike the Sequalitchew Creek Trail, 64

INDEX

27 West, 113

253 Collective Art Gallery, 131

ALMA, 44

America's Car Museum, 41

Anderson Island, 59

Arcade, 52

Art Glass, 12, 45, 84, 88, 98, 102

Art House Café, 3

Banchan, 10, 19

Bob's Java Jive, 46

Brown and Haley Factory Store, 125

Browns Point Lighthouse Park, 100

Buffalo Soldiers Museum, 87

Bullseye Lane Axe Throwing, 48

Business and Historic Districts, 91

Chambers Bay, 57

Chambers Bay Golf Course, 57

Chambers Creek Regional Park, 69

Charlotte's Blueberry Park, 77

Chihuly Bridge of Glass, 88

Coffee, 8, 86, 119

Commencement Bay 2, 62, 89

Compass Rose, 122

Copper & Salt Northwest Kitchen, 2

Craft Cocktail 2, 6, 11, 40

Crystal Mountain Resort, 70

Cuerno Bravo Prime Steakhouse and
 Cantina, 13

D Haberdashery, 129

Dale Chihuly 84, 85, 88, 98, 102

Dorky's, 52

Duke's Seafood, 28–29

Dune Peninsula Park, 66

Dupont, 96–97

Dupont Historical Museum, 96

El Gaucho, 4

Emerald Queen Event Center, 42

Escape Hour, 39

Farm-to-Table, 12

Farmers Market, 33, 74, 127

Farrell Marsh, 68

Fort Nisqually Living History
 Museum, 92–93

Fort Steilacoom Park, 74

Foss Waterway Seaport, 90

Freighthouse Square, 116–117

Frisko Freeze, 16

Gig Harbor, 25, 32, 105, 119

Gig Harbor Gondola, 32

Golf, 57

Hi-Voltage Records and Books, 49

Homestead Restaurant & Bakery, 26

Hotel Murano, 102

Ice Cream Social, 14

Incalmo, 12

Jan Parker Cookery, 5

Jazzbones, 47

Job Carr Cabin Museum, 104

Johnson Candy Company, 126

Karpeles Manuscript Museum, 106

Katie Downs, 28–29

Keys on Main, 50

Kindship, 120

King's Books, 130

Legendary Doughnuts, 7

LeMay Collections at Marymount, 36

Lewis Army Museum, 94

Lobster Shop, 28–29

Marzano, 22–23

Marvel Food and Deli, 22–23

McCormick Forest Park, 76

McMenamins Elks Temple, 34–35

Metropolitan Market, 24–25

Mount Rainier, 70–71

Museum of Glass, 84, 88

New Gangnam BBQ, 19

Northwest Trek, 72

Ocean5, 40

Old Town Tacoma 28, 104

Olive Branch Café, 116

Olympic Mountains 2, 28, 33, 64, 78, 118

Pacific Northwest Shop, 127

Pal Do World, 10

Parkland, 22–23

Parkland Place Bakery and Bistro, 22–23

Pine and Moss, 112

Point Defiance Park 24, 63

Point Defiance Zoo and Aquarium, 58

Point Ruston, 63, 66

Point Ruston Public Market, 118

Pretty Gritty Tours, 38

Puget Sound, 78

Puyallup Tribe Walk, 67

Ruston Way, 28, 29

Sanford and Son Antiques, 24

Sequalitchew Creek Trail, 64

Shin Shin, 114

Sixth Avenue District 20, 47

Stadium District, 3

Stanford's Steak, 11

Steak, 4, 11, 13, 26

Steilacoom, 59, 68, 78

Steilacoom Farmers Market, 33

Steilacoom Historical Museum, 108

Sunnyside Beach, 78–79

Swan Creek Park, 80

Table 47, 6

Tacoma Art Museum, 85

Tacoma Book Center, 128

Tacoma Chinese Reconciliation Park, 89

Tacoma Comedy Club, 51

Tacoma Dome, 41

Tacoma Glass Studio, 45

Tacoma Museum District, 11

Tacoma Narrows Bridge, 60–61, 105

Tacoma Nature Center, 65

Tacoma Night Market, 53

Tacoma Rainiers, 56

Tacoma Theater District, 43

Thea Foss Waterway, 62, 88

Thornewood Castle, 101

Tibbitts Fernhill, 18

Tickled Pink, 123

Tinkertopia, 132

Titlow Park & Lodge, 78–79
Topside Coffee Cabin, 8–9
Trail, 64–69, 74, 76, 78, 80
Tricky's Pop Culture Emporium, 133
Union Station, 98
Uptown Gig Harbor, 119

War Memorial Park, 60
Washington State History Museum, 86
Watson's Greenhouse and Nursery, 115
Wheel Fun Rentals, 63
Wilson Way Bridge, 66
W.W. Seymour Botanical Conservatory, 107